THE WEB WIZARD'S GUIDE TO PHOTOSHOP®

SHERRY HUTSON

PEARSON

Addison Wesley

Boston   San Francisco   New York
London Toronto Sydney Tokyo Singapore Madrid
Mexico City Munich Paris Cape Town Hong Kong Montreal

Senior Acquisitions Editor: *Michael Hirsch*
Project Editor: *Maite Suarez-Rivas*
Senior Production Supervisor: *Juliet Silveri*
Marketing Manager: *Michelle Brown*
Production Packaging Services: *Gillian Hall, The Aardvark Group*
Copyeditor: *Penelope Hull*
Proofreader: *Holly McLean-Aldis*
Cover and Interior Designer: *Leslie Haimes*
Text and Cover Design Supervisor: *Gina Hagen Kolenda/Joyce Cosentino Wells*
Print Buyer: *Caroline Fell*

Access the latest information about Addison-Wesley titles from our World Wide Web site: *http://www.aw-bc.com/computing*

Many of the designations used by manufacturers and sellers to distinguish their products are claimed as trademarks. Where those designations appear in this book, and Addison-Wesley was aware of a trademark claim, the designations have been printed in initial caps or all caps.

The programs and applications presented in this book have been included for their instructional value. They have been tested with care, but are not guaranteed for any particular purpose. The publisher does not offer any warranties or representations, nor does it accept any liabilities with respect to the programs or applications.

Library of Congress Cataloging-in-Publication Data
Hutson, Sherry.
   The Web Wizard's guide to Photoshop / Sherry Hutson.
       p. cm. -- (Addison-Wesley's Web wizard series)
   ISBN 0-321-24727-2
   1. Computer graphics. 2. Adobe Photoshop. 3. Web sites--Design. I. Title. II.
Series.

T385.H889 2004
006.6'86--dc22   2004044444

For information on obtaining permission for the use of material from this work, please submit a written request to Pearson Education, Inc., Rights and Contracts Department, 75 Arlington St., Suite 300, Boston, MA 02116 or fax your request to 617-848-7047.

12345678910—QWT—060504

TABLE OF CONTENTS

Preface   ix

Chapter One   **PHOTOSHOP: FAST START FOR BEGINNERS** 1

Key Features in Photoshop 2
     Creating Images 2
     Editing Images 3
     Using Layers 3
     Making Web Pages 3
     Advanced Features 3

Work Area 4
     Menu Bar 4
     Options Bar (or Palettes) 5
     Toolbox 5
     Palettes 6
     Arranging Your Work Area 6
     Setting Preferences 6

Designing with Color 7
     Photoshop's Color Modes 7
     Color Tools in the Toolbox 8
     Using the Color Picker 8
     Using the Color and Swatches Palettes 10
     Setting Up Your Work Area with Web-Safe Color 11
     General Information about Color Tools 12
     Color Harmony for the Web .13

Using the Painting Tools to Make a Color Guide 13
     Creating and Coloring a New Image 14
     Harmonious Color Schemes .15
     Tools and Techniques for Choosing and Saving Colors 16

Saving Your Images in the Correct Format for the Web 17
     Save Menu Commands 18
     Guidelines for Saving and Naming Images 18
     Using the Three Save Commands 20
     Saving a GIF Image for the Web 23

Summary 24 ✯ *Online References 24* ✯
Review Questions 24 ✯ *Hands-On Exercises 25*

Chapter Two | AQUIRING AND EDITING IMAGES 27

Scanning 28

    General Principles for Scanning .28

    Ways to Acquire Images Besides Scanning 29

Editing an Image: The Basic Tools 30

    Saving a Scanned Image 30

    Saving a Copy of an Image 30

    Rotating the Canvas 31

    Cropping an Image 31

    Adjusting Black and White Levels 32

    Adjusting the Colors 33

    Sharpening the Image 35

Image Size and Resolution 35

    What Is a Pixel? 35

    Rationale for the Saving Strategy 36

    Using the Image Size Box 36

    Relationship Between Pixels, Image Size, and Resolution . .38

    Monitor Resolution and the Web 39

    Common Image Sizes for the Web 39

Editing Your Image: Fun with Photoshop 40

    Using Filters 40

    Using the Selection Tools 41

    Clone Stamp Tool 43

    Advanced Editing Tools 44

    Using Photoshop Appropriately .44

Saving a JPG Image for the Web 44

    About Compression 45

    Using the Save for Web Command 45

Summary 47 ✲ Online References 47 ✲
Review Questions 47 ✲ Hands-On Exercises 48

Chapter Three | CREATING GRAPHIC IMAGES 49

General Information About Graphic Images 50

    Raster (Bitmap) Versus Vector Images 50

    More Essentials About Color, GIF, and JPG Images 51

Using Transparency 54

    Setting Up Your Work Area for Using Transparency 54

    Creating a New Transparent Image 54

    Drawing a Vector Image 54

Basic Tools for Creating Web Graphics .56
    Using the Shape Tools for Vector Graphics 56
    Using the Pen Tools 58
    Using the Styles Palette 61
    Transforming Shapes 62
    Using the Painting Tools for Raster Graphics 63
Saving a Graphic with a Transparent Background for the Web 64
    Using Matte When Saving a Transparent GIF File 65

Summary 67 ✧ *Online References 67* ✧
Review Questions 67 ✧ *Hands-On Exercises 68*

Chapter Four   **USING TEXT, LAYERS, EFFECTS, AND STYLES** 69

Text on the Web: Basic Principles 70
    Live Text 70
    Image Text 70
    Text on the Screen Versus Text on the Printed Page 71
Text Tool in Photoshop 72
    Using the Text Tool 72
    Single-Line Text and Paragraph Text 76
    Using the Character Palette 76
    Using the Paragraph Palette 76
Using Layers 77
    Background Layer 78
    Adding, Deleting, and Naming Layers 78
    Selecting Layers 80
    Showing and Hiding Layers 80
    Duplicating Layers 81
    Moving Layers 81
    Moving the Contents of Layers .81
Using Effects and Styles 82
    Drop Shadow Effect 82
    Bevel and Emboss Effect 84
    Other Effects 86
    Saving a Custom Style 86
Compositing an Image 87
Saving a Layered Image 90

Summary 91 ✧ *Online References 91* ✧
Review Questions 91 ✧ *Hands-On Exercises 92*

Chapter Five   MAKING A WEB ANIMATION 93
Basic Principles of Animation 94
    Animated GIF Images 94
Using ImageReady 95
Creating a Basic Animation 96
    Animated Advertising Banners for the Web 96
    Creating Layers for Animation 98
    Creating Frames of Animation 99
    Timing the Animation 103
Creating a Complex Animation 104
    Animation in Place 105
    Animation in Place and Along a Path 106
Optimizing and Saving Your Animation for the Web 109
    Optimize Animation Menu Command 109
    Optimize Palette 109
    Tabs at the Top of the Document Window 110
    Saving Your Animation 111
Summary 112 ✿ Online References 112 ✿
Review Questions 112 ✿ Hands-On Exercises 113

Chapter Six   DESIGNING A WEB PAGE 115
Web Design Basics 116
Using Photoshop and ImageReady to Design a Web Page . . .118
Designing a Web Page 119
    Creating a New Document to Match the
    Size of Your Web Page 120
    Visually Dividing the Design Area into
    Rows and Columns 120
    Using Symbols and Metaphors to Help
    Determine Your Design 121
    Designing Navigation 123
    Designing Above the Fold 124
    Sketching Design Layouts 125
Backgrounds and Simple Rollovers 125
    Creating Background Graphics and Tiles 126
    Using ImageReady to Preview a Background
    Tile in a Browser 128
    Setting Up a Simple Rollover Behavior in Photoshop 129
Saving a Showpeg 131
Summary 132 ✿ Online References 132 ✿
Review Questions 132 ✿ Hands-On Exercises 133

Chapter Seven   **PUBLISHING YOUR WEB PAGE** 135
          Slicing a Web Page 136
                Learning to Use Slices 136
                Creating Slices 138
                Slices from Guides 139
                Setting Slice Options 141
                Live Web Text 144
          Using the Optimize Settings 146
          Creating Rollover Behavior .147
                Programming a Rollover Behavior 147
                Using Prebuilt Rollover Styles 148
          Using Simple Image Maps 149
          Setting the Output Options .150
                Saving Background Colors or Images 151
          Saving a Web Page 152
          Summary 155 ✥ *Online References 155* ✥
          Review Questions 156 ✥ *Hands-On Exercises 156*

Chapter Eight   **BEYOND THE BASICS** 157
          Getting Help 158
          Tools, Tips, and Techniques .158
                Actions 158
                Blending Modes 159
                Canvas Size 159
                Color Replacement Tool .160
                Contact Sheet 160
                Design 162
                Directory Structure 162
                Disjointed (or Remote) Rollovers 162
                Docking Bar (Palette Well) 163
                Drop Caps 164
                Drop Shadows and Other Layer Effects 164
                Duplicate Layer 165
                Export to Macromedia Flash (SWF) 165
                Extract Background 165
                Feathering 166
                File Browser 167
                File Size 167
                Full Screen Mode 168
                Gradients 168

Grayscale 168
Healing Brush 169
Inverse—Selecting 169
Lasso Tools—Polygon and Magnetic Tools 170
Layer Comps 170
Liquify 170
Live Text 170
Locking Layers 171
Master Originals Folder 171
Merging Layers 171
Opacity 171
Pattern Maker 171
Quick Mask 172
Rasterizing Text Layers 173
Red Eye Correction 173
Retouching Tools 174
Style Guide 174
Tile Maker 175
Web Photo Gallery 175
WBMP Format for Cell Phones and PDAs 175
Web Site Design Do's and Don'ts .175
Summary 177 ✢ Online References 177 ✢
Review Questions 177 ✢ Hands-On Exercises 177

Appendix   ANSWERS TO ODD-NUMBERED REVIEW QUESTIONS 179

Index 185

Credits 191

Web-Safe Colors 197

ImageReady© CS Toolbox . . . . .Final page

Photoshop© CS Toolbox . . . . .Inside back cover

PREFACE

About Addison-Wesley's Web Wizard Series

The beauty of the Web is that, with a little effort, anyone can harness its power to create sophisticated Web sites. *Addison-Wesley's Web Wizard Series* helps readers master the Web by presenting a concise introduction to one important Internet topic or technology in each book. The books start from square one and assume no prior experience with the technology being covered. Mastering the Web doesn't come with a wave of a magic wand, but by studying these accessible, highly visual textbooks, readers will be well on their way.

The series is written by instructors familiar with the challenges beginners face when first learning the material. To this end, the Web Wizard books offer more than a cookbook approach: they emphasize principles and offer clear explanations, giving the reader a strong foundation of knowledge on which to build.

Numerous features highlight important points and aid in learning:

☆ Tips—important points to keep in mind

☆ Shortcuts—time-saving ideas

☆ Warnings—things to watch out for

☆ Review questions and hands-on exercises

☆ Online references—Web sites to visit for more information

Supplements

Supplementary materials for the books, including updates, additional examples, and sample files are available at `http://www.aw-bc.com/webwizard`. Additional supplements for instructors adopting a book from the series include: instructors' manuals, test banks, PowerPoint slides, solutions, and Course Compass—a dynamic online course management system powered by Blackboard. Instructors should contact the local Addison-Wesley sales representative for access to these.

About This Book

Adobe Photoshop—and its companion application ImageReady—is the premier program for creating and editing images for print, the Web, and emerging media. This book is an introduction to using Photoshop for the Web. No previous experience with the program is required. Dozens of screenshots and step-by-step instructions illustrate a variety of techniques applicable to multiple versions of the program, including the latest release, Photoshop CS.

Though it began as an image editing program, Photoshop has evolved into a full-featured Web publishing program that has revolutionized the way Web pages are created. In this book, you will learn how to edit photographs for a Web site and produce original Web logos, buttons, and animations. You also will learn how to design and publish complete Web pages without needing to use a Web editor or do any HTML coding.

In addition to the exercises in each chapter, the book includes sections on color harmony, ethics and Photoshop, graphic design basics, and Web design theory. Also included is a Do's and Don'ts list for effective Web design, and a collection of advanced tools, tips, and techniques that take the beginner to the next level of competence. Appendices include a Web-Safe Colors chart, and charts of commonly used tools and keyboard shortcuts.

Acknowledgments

I am indebted to the hundreds of students who have taken my classes over the years. Their creative spirits and motivation to learn difficult material have inspired me, and I have consistently learned as much as I've taught.

I would like to thank Emily Genaway, who originally approached me about this project, and Michael Hirsch who made it happen. And many thanks to Maite Suarez-Rivas, Lesly Hershman, Joyce Wells, and Juliet Silveri at Addison-Wesley—as well as Penny Hull and Gillian Hall—who guided me through the process and produced a beautiful book.

I am also grateful to the reviewers whose wise comments and suggestions improved the book. My thanks go to Diane Dallis at Indiana University Bloomington, Tina Spain McDuffie, author of *Javascript Concepts & Techniques*; Cindy Royal of the University of Texas at Austin; Mark Douglas from the Fontbonne University; Wayne Knowles of Chemeketa Community College; Sara L. Cloutier from Sonoma State University; Peggy Jones at MiraCosta College; John Sappington; Dave L. Dion; Vanessa Dennen; Lawrence Goetz; and anonymous reviewers from the College of Visual Arts, NWACC, and Ohio State.

I am forever indebted to Ed Wojcicki—a great editor and a great friend—and especially to Stephanie, Tim, Marlene, Bill, Lynn, Channing, Chris, and Nikki, whose encouragement and support made this possible.

Finally, this book is dedicated to Samantha, Madeline, and Tyler—the next generation of Photoshop users.

Sherry Hutson
May 2004

CHAPTER ONE

PHOTOSHOP: FAST START FOR BEGINNERS

This chapter introduces you to Photoshop and prepares you to create images for the Web. It begins with an overview of features and an explanation of the work area. Then it explains basic concepts to help you understand the role of color harmony in effective Web design. You will use Photoshop's tools to create a color guide—a selection of colors for your Web site. You will also learn how to save your images in the proper format for your Web site. Even if you are a complete novice, this book will get you up and running quickly.

Chapter Objectives

☆ Learn the wide variety of tasks you can perform with Photoshop

☆ Understand some of the tools you'll use most often as a beginner

☆ Become acquainted with using color in Photoshop

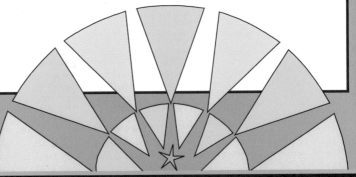

Key Features in Photoshop

☆ Consider the importance of choosing the right colors for your Web site

☆ Save images in the correct format for the Web

◎◎ Key Features in Photoshop

Adobe Photoshop is the premier program for creating and editing compelling images. Along with its companion program, ImageReady, you can use Photoshop to produce your work for print, emerging media such as wireless devices, and the Web.

This book focuses on the creation of images for the Web.

You may have always used the word *picture* to describe a photograph, a work of art, a graphic, a logo, or a number of other things that contain visual representations. As a Photoshop Web designer, you should use the word **image** to describe these things.

An image can contain colors, geometric shapes, text, photographs, drawings, cartoons, line art, illustrations, clip art, animations, or any kind of symbol of a person, place, or thing.

If you are new to image making and Web design, begin to think of yourself as an *artist*, who uses *paint* and *brushes*, or a *photographer*, who uses a *camera* and a *darkroom* to create original images. With Photoshop, you will do these things on a computer. This section of Chapter One gives you an overview of the many features of Photoshop that you will learn about in this book.

Do not panic if you see an occasional term that you do not recognize in this opening chapter. Each term will be explained clearly in the step-by-step sections of the book.

Creating Images

There are several ways to create an image in Photoshop:

☆ You can start with a blank page, or *canvas*, and use any of various tools to paint, draw, add text and other images, and apply artistic effects.

☆ You can open an image you've saved from a clip art or photo collection.

☆ You can open an image you've saved from the Web.

☆ You can open a "screenshot" you've captured from your computer.

☆ You can use Photoshop to scan a photograph, a drawing, or an object.

☆ You can download an image from a digital camera.

You will begin creating images as you read this chapter, and you will continue to do so throughout your study of the book.

☆ **WARNING** **Don't Use the Work of Others**

Though it is simple to save virtually any image you find on a Web site or scan an image from a book or magazine, it is not always a considerate or legal thing to do. Beware of taking original, copyrighted works that do not belong to you and using them as your own.

Editing Images

Photoshop gives you powerful tools for cropping, resizing, retouching, rotating, flipping, and otherwise transforming your image. An assortment of selection tools lets you select all or a part of your image and then make a change that applies only to the part you've selected. You can paint and draw on top of or under the image, and you can make duplicates of all or part of your image. You can use type to add a large, colorful headline or a body of text. Photoshop also includes many simple ways to produce dazzling effects. You will begin to learn editing techniques in Chapter Two.

Photoshop allows you to create *painted*, or **raster**, images as well as *drawn*, or **vector**, images. You will learn more about the difference between raster and vector images in Chapter Three.

Using Layers

If you've ever used tracing paper, you have an idea of how **layers** work. For example, a layered Photoshop image might have one layer containing a photograph, another layer with a photo caption, and another layer with a large headline at the top of the photo. Though these layers appear merged together when the final file is used for print or the Web, they are organized as distinct levels while you are editing the image. This gives you complete control over each element of your image. You can edit one layer without changing any of the other layers. You can choose to "see through" all or part of the layers. You will learn how to use layers in Chapter Four.

Making Web Pages

With Photoshop and its companion program, **ImageReady**, you can create individual elements for a Web site or you can design an entire Web page with graphics, photos, and text. You can add animations for Web buttons or other images. You can even specify areas that are not images and will contain *live* Web text. When your page is complete, you can slice it up to assure speedy download times and save all the images along with the Hypertext Markup Language (HTML) file that is necessary for viewing in a Web browser. You can also save your images for use with a Web editor software program like Adobe Go Live, Macromedia Dreamweaver, or Microsoft Front Page.

You will learn to create an animation in Chapter Five. You will use Photoshop to design and save a complete Web page—or just the images for the page—in Chapters Six and Seven.

Advanced Features

Photoshop has many advanced features that this book will not address. Photoshop is a program so deep in capability that one person would be hard-pressed to learn it all.

The goal of this book is to get you up and running. You will learn to use the basic tools you need to prepare images for the Web.

Chapter Eight includes tips for using some of Photoshop's advanced features—after you have mastered the techniques presented in the first seven chapters.

◎◎ Work Area

Photoshop includes a Menu bar (A), an Options bar (B), a Toolbox (C), and palettes (D) to give you all the tools you need to create and edit images. You can "Show" and "Hide" these components as needed while you are working. As you read the following section, refer to Figure 1.1, which shows the Photoshop work area.

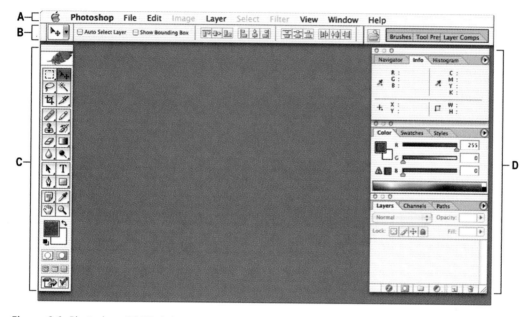

Figure 1.1 Photoshop CS Work Area

☆ **TIP   Open Photoshop and Follow Along**

It will be helpful for you to open Photoshop on your computer and follow along with the material in this book. Later in this chapter and in subsequent chapters, you will create and edit images and apply the techniques presented in the chapters.

Menu Bar

The Menu bar across the top of the screen organizes menus for performing particular tasks. In each menu, you will find commands for working with the particular menu task. For example, the File and Edit menus contain familiar commands like New, Open, Save, Copy, and Paste. The other menus may appear strange to you. You will learn certain specific menu commands as you go along. The goal is to learn only what you need to know to get up and running.

Options Bar (or Palettes)

Most of the tools in Photoshop have *options* that are displayed in the Options bar (below the Menu bar at the top of the screen). These options allow you to vary certain settings so that you can get precisely the effect you wish when editing your image. (In older versions of Photoshop, options are displayed on palettes rather than on an option bar.)

Toolbox

The Toolbox contains tools to create and edit images. You select a tool by clicking on it once. It will appear depressed, which means that it is the active tool. Some of the tool icons have additional tools hidden behind them. To view these tools, click and hold on the tool icon. You will see the additional tools. Click on the one you want and it will become the active tool. Figure 1.2 shows the Toolbox, along with the names of the tools. Keyboard shortcuts for selecting individual tools are shown in parentheses. On the inside back cover of this book is an extended version of the Toolbox, including the submenus that appear under some of the tools.

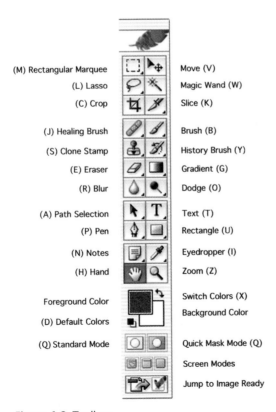

(M) Rectangular Marquee	Move (V)
(L) Lasso	Magic Wand (W)
(C) Crop	Slice (K)
(J) Healing Brush	Brush (B)
(S) Clone Stamp	History Brush (Y)
(E) Eraser	Gradient (G)
(R) Blur	Dodge (O)
(A) Path Selection	Text (T)
(P) Pen	Rectangle (U)
(N) Notes	Eyedropper (I)
(H) Hand	Zoom (Z)
Foreground Color	Switch Colors (X)
(D) Default Colors	Background Color
(Q) Standard Mode	Quick Mask Mode (Q)
	Screen Modes
	Jump to Image Ready

Figure 1.2 Toolbox

☆**TIP**   **Tool Tips**

At first, it is difficult to memorize all the icons for the tools. If you move your pointer over the top of a particular tool, a box will pop up and display the tool's name. This box is called a **Tool Tip**. Tool Tips are available for most of the icons and boxes in the Photoshop work area. As you read this book, you can also refer to the illustration on the inside back cover as a reminder of the names of the tools in the Toolbox.

Palettes

Palettes are boxes that contain information and settings that help you edit your image. Each palette contains tabs along the top. When you click a tab, the information or settings for the tab's menu item come to the front. Most palettes also contain an additional menu. You can see this menu by pressing the side-pointing triangle in the upper right corner of the palette.

☆**WARNING**   **About Palettes**

The word *palette* is used in two different ways. A set of particular colors is often referred to as a *palette*, similar to the device a painter uses. Photoshop refers to its many boxes of tools and information in the work area as *palettes*.

Arranging Your Work Area

When you open Photoshop for the first time, the Options bar appears horizontally across the top, under the Menu bar. The Toolbox appears in the upper left corner of the screen. The palettes appear on the right side of the screen, stacked on top of each other. (See Figure 1.1.)

You can move any of these items (except for the Menu bar) by clicking on the top bar of the item and dragging it to the location of your choice. You can "Show" or "Hide" the items by choosing Window in the Menu bar and dragging your mouse down to highlight the item. When the item is on the desktop, it appears in the list with a checkmark beside it.

Setting Preferences

In addition to arranging the work area, you can set several **preferences** that affect the way the program displays certain information. For now, we will set one of the preferences related to images for the Web.

1. In the Menu bar, choose Edit and drag down to Preferences. In the menu that appears to the right, choose Units and Rulers.

2. In the box that appears, find the pop-up box next to Rulers in the Units area. Choose Pixels in the pop-up box.

3. Click OK to return to the desktop.

A pixel is the smallest unit of measurement for images shown on a computer monitor. Thus, pixels are the most-often-used unit of measurement for Web images. You may be more familiar with inches as a unit of measurement, but as a Web designer, you should learn to work with pixels.

◎◎ Designing with Color

Using color effectively is perhaps one of the most important considerations for a designer. Most novices have never given much thought to color and tend to choose colors randomly. As a Web designer, your color choices can make the difference between an ordinary Web page and one that appears compelling, well-thought-out, and integrated with the goals of the site and the audience. This chapter concentrates on color. You will learn to think about color before you begin to design, and you will make a guide that defines the color scheme for your Web page.

Photoshop contains many tools and settings for use with color. This book deals specifically with Photoshop for the Web, so you will learn only the tools available to create images for Web pages.

Photoshop's Color Modes

Photoshop includes several **color modes**, or methods of using and displaying color. As a Web designer, you are concerned with only three of Photoshop's modes.

In the Menu bar, choose Mode. A pop-up box shows the list of modes available.

Here are the three color modes you are most likely to use for Web images:

☆ **Grayscale** is a color mode that includes black, white, and shades of gray. When you refer to "black and white photos," you are probably really referring to grayscale photos.

☆ **Indexed Color** is a color mode that is made up of no more than 256 specific colors. Images that use an indexed color mode are referred to as having an index palette. There can be many different index palettes with many sets of 256 indexed colors.

☆ **RGB Color** is a color mode that includes red, green, and blue. These are the colors that a computer monitor (or a television screen) uses to display color. You get different colors, like orange, purple, and yellow, by mixing red, green, and blue in different combinations.

Among the color modes shown in the Mode pop-up box is CMYK. This mode is used for printing and is not used in this book. If you are using an image that was previously prepared for print in the CMYK color mode, you can change the color mode to RGB to prepare the image for the Web.

If it is not already chosen in the Image➜Mode menu, choose RGB as the color mode.

Designing with Color

Color Tools in the Toolbox

If you look in the lower area of the Toolbox, you will see two squares that overlap each other. These are the Color Selection boxes that represent colors that are the active colors. They are referred to as the Foreground Color (top) and Background Color (bottom). Sometimes these color boxes are referred to as *chips*. Figure 1.3 shows the Color Selection boxes in the Toolbox.

Figure 1.3 Color Selection Boxes

When you open Photoshop for the first time, the Foreground Color box is black and the Background Color box is white. These are the default colors. You will change the colors in just a moment. If you ever want to get back to the default colors, you can click the icon near the lower left of the boxes (it looks like a miniature of the boxes).

If you want to reverse the order of the boxes—make white the foreground color and black the background color—you can click the icon near the top right of the boxes (it looks like a curved arrow with two heads).

If they are not already the active colors, choose black foreground and white background colors now by clicking on the lower left icon (the miniature Color Selection boxes).

☆ **TIP**   **Shortcut for Choosing the Default Colors**

If you've set up other colors in your Foreground Color and Background Color selection boxes and you wish to quickly revert to black and white, press the D key on the keyboard.

Using the Color Picker

If you click on the Foreground Color box, a box called the Color Picker will appear: Refer to Figure 1.4 as you read the following explanation of the Color Picker box.

☆ On the left side is a large square containing variations of colors where you can pick colors by clicking with your mouse.

☆ At the bottom left is a checkbox labeled Only Web Colors. When this box is checked, a limited number of colors called the Web 216 will be available. The Web 216 is explained later in more detail.

⭐ Down the middle is a column that also contains various colors, with two opposing arrowheads at the bottom on either side of the column.

⭐ On the right side are several boxes within which you can click and enter numbers that define colors.

⭐ In the top right you see buttons for OK, Cancel, and Custom. Click OK after you've selected a new color and wish to make it active. Click Cancel to close the color box without changing the active color. Custom is a box used primarily by print designers, and you will not use this button.

⭐ Near the top, between the column and the buttons, is a box that shows two colors: the color you've picked is in the top half; the color that is currently the active color in the Toolbox is in the bottom half.

Click in several different locations in the large square. Notice that the numbers in the various boxes on the right side change. Every color has a unique *code* made up of numbers and/or letters. This is a good thing for designers, because it makes it easy to remember exactly which color you want to use from one design session to the next.

Choose a color in the large square and click OK to exit the Color Picker.

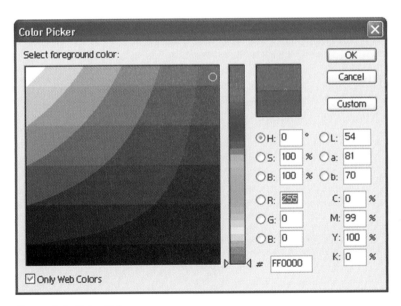

Figure 1.4 Color Picker

Using the Color and Swatches Palettes

Besides the Color Picker, there are other ways to choose particular colors in Photoshop. If the Color palette is not already open, go to the Window menu and choose Color. The work area palette labeled Color appears. Figure 1.5 shows the Color palette.

☆**TIP**   **Window Menu**

The items in the WIndow menu are either *on* or *off*. When they are *on*, they appear in the list with a checkbox beside them, and they are visible on the desktop.

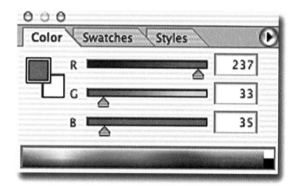

Figure 1.5 Color Palette

Using the Color Palette Spectrum

☆ At the top left of the Color palette is a small reproduction of the Color Selection boxes from the Toolbox.

☆ There are bars across the middle called slider bars. If you chose RGB from the Image→Mode menu earlier, then these bars are labeled R, G, and B. On the right are boxes where you can view and/or change the codes for each color bar.

☆ Across the bottom is a **spectrum**, or range, of color with bits of red, green, blue, and other colors.

When you hold your mouse over the spectrum, the pointer becomes an eyedropper. If you click an area with the eyedropper, you are picking a foreground color. You will see the color in the color selection boxes, and you will see the indicators under each of the center bars change position. Then you will see different codes, or numbers, appear in each of the boxes to the right. When you select a color in the Color palette, it becomes the active color in the Toolbox.

You can also move the slider bars manually to select a color, or you can enter numbers directly into the boxes.

Using the Swatches Palette

Next to the Color tab in the palette, you should see a tab labeled Swatches. Click the tab to reveal the Swatches palette. If you do not see the Swatches tab, go to the Window menu and select Swatches. Figure 1.6 shows the Swatches palette.

The Swatches palette contains small boxes, or **swatches**, of color. When you move your mouse over any of the small boxes of color in the Swatches palette, the pointer becomes an eyedropper. Click on a box of color with the eyedropper to select that particular color. When you select a color in the Swatches palette, it becomes the active color in the Toolbox and in the Color palette.

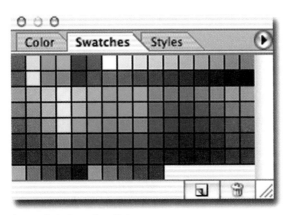

Figure 1.6 Swatches Palette

Setting Up Your Work Area with Web-Safe Color

At the time Hypertext Markup Language (HTML) and the World Wide Web were invented, most computer monitors were capable of displaying only 256 specific colors on the screen. Those colors were chosen because they displayed uniformly on most computer monitors.

Forty of those colors were reserved for the computer's operating system displays, leaving 216 colors for the text, backgrounds, and graphics associated with documents and programs. That particular set of colors is referred to as the **Web 216**.

In the early years of the Web, designers used only colors from the Web 216. They knew those colors would display uniformly for most users.

For most designers, the Web 216 (also known as the Web-safe colors) now seems restrictive. Today's computer monitors are capable of displaying millions of colors uniformly, and Web designers no longer use the Web 216 exclusively. However, many of the emerging portable wireless devices, such as PDAs, cell phones, and pagers, are capable of displaying only a limited set of colors or grays on the screen. So Web designers are still concerned about color choices.

For beginning designers, it may be easier to use the Web 216—a limited selection of colors—as your color palette for the exercises in this book. See the second-to-last page of this book for a chart of all Web 216 colors.

Using the Web 216 and the Color Palette

At the top right of the Color palette, you'll see a small circle with a triangle pointing to the right ⦿. This is a menu button.

1. Click the menu button to see a pop-up menu that contains a list of items that refer to the types of images you can produce. Select Web Color Sliders.

2. Move the sliders around and notice that some numbers and letters, like 99, 66, CC, and FF, appear in the boxes on the right. These numbers and letters are **hexadecimal** codes that define the colors in the Web 216.

Using the Web 216 and the Swatches Palette

1. Select the Swatches palette and click the menu button.

2. Select Web Safe Colors from the pop-up list. Notice the selection of colors that becomes available in the Swatches palette.

Using the Web 216 and the Color Picker

1. Click on top of the foreground color chip in the Toolbox to reveal the Color Picker.

2. Check the box in the lower left corner labeled Only Web Colors. When this box is checked, only colors from the Web 216 will be available.

General Information about Color Tools

The colors you choose when you use the Color Picker or the Color or Swatches palettes will apply to all images you create with various tools like the Brush tool or the Text tool.

When setting up your Color and Swatches palettes, if you do not wish to use the Web Color sliders, choose the RGB sliders. RGB is the color mode used for images that will be displayed on the Web (as opposed to print). The RGB color mode contains many colors in addition to the Web 216. Think of the Web 216 as a subset of all RGB colors.

The Web 216 colors—called hexadecimal codes—have corresponding RGB codes. See the chart of Web 216 colors on the second-to-last page of this book. The chart includes both hexadecimal and RGB codes for each of the colors.

☆ **TIP**   **What's a Hexadecimal?**

Sometimes computers use a numbering system that represents digits greater than 9 as letters. This is a hexadecimal numbering system. As with all colors, each color in the Web 216 has a unique code. The codes for Web 216 colors are expressed as hexadecimals, that is, combinations of numbers and letters. This is useful to designers for remembering exact colors used from one project to the next.

Color Harmony for the Web

You've probably seen lots of Web sites, and you may or may not have paid attention to the colors used for backgrounds, buttons, boxes, and other elements of the sites. As a Web designer, you should look at Web sites with particular attention to color and pleasing combinations of color.

Theoreticians have studied color from the beginning of time. Some believe that different colors evoke different emotions. Trend spotters claim to note the mood of the people and thus announce the most favorable colors for the coming year of fashion and design. Schools of design often teach that certain colors provoke certain responses:

☆ Red may be hot and exciting.

☆ Blue may be cold and icy.

☆ Orange and yellow may be warm and inviting.

☆ Green and turquoise may be soothing and calm.

Color values, also known as their lightness or darkness, are also important to designers:

☆ Light or pale colors may be gentle and relaxing.

☆ Dark colors may be serious and make spaces seem closed.

☆ Bright colors may be exhilarating attention getters, and they are often used in design for children.

Contrast is perhaps one of the most important considerations for a Web designer. High-contrast images—for example, thick, black letters on a white background—make content more readable and visual images pop off the page. Beware of making Web sites that do not include enough contrast—for example, thin red letters on a black background are hard to read.

◎◎ Using the Painting Tools to Make a Color Guide

Before you design your images for the Web, consider the goal of your Web site, the audience you are trying to reach, and the results you wish to achieve by using color on your site.

Make your best attempt to choose the right colors, even though you can never be absolutely sure how color is viewed on different monitors, by different people, or in different situations.

Using the Color tools in Photoshop, you can create a guide for the colors you will use in your Web site.

In this section, you will learn how to do the following:

1. Create a new Photoshop image.

2. Choose colors for a Web site by creating a color guide.

3. Save your color guide as a GIF image for the Web.

Creating and Coloring a New Image

Go to the File menu and choose New. The New box opens with several areas where you can make choices:

1. At the top, type a Name for your image. Use lowercase letters, with no spaces, and keep it brief—for example: colorGuide. (You'll learn more about how to name your files later.)

2. In the box labeled Width, type the number 200. In the pop-up box to the right, make sure the selection is Pixels. If not, click the pop-up and choose Pixels.

3. In the box labeled Height, type the number 200. In the pop-up box to the right, make sure the selection is Pixels. If not, click the pop-up and choose Pixels.

4. In the box labeled Resolution, type the number 72. Make sure the selection in the pop-up box is Pixels/inch. You'll learn more about resolution in Chapter Two.

5. In the pop-up box labeled Mode, make sure the selection is RGB color.

6. At the bottom, in the area labeled Contents (called Background Contents in newer versions of Photoshop), click White.

7. When you are finished, click the OK button.

You've just created an image. It is 200 pixels wide by 200 pixels high. Its resolution and color mode are prepared for Web editing, and it contains white as the background color.

The image is a blank canvas, and you are the artist. You'll use Photoshop's tools to fill your canvas with color.

Follow these procedures to learn how to use the Fill technique and the Brush tool.

Using the Fill Technique

1. Use any of the color selection (or picking) tools—the Color Picker, the Color palette, or the Swatches palette—to pick a color.

2. Go to the Edit menu and choose Fill.

3. In the pop-up box labeled Use, choose Foreground Color. Leave the other items in the Fill box at the default values.

4. Click OK. The image will be filled with the foreground color.

You've painted on your canvas using the Fill technique.

As with most computer programs, you can use the Edit→Undo menu if you change your mind. Choose Undo now in order to proceed with this exercise.

1. Click on the Brush tool in the Toolbox (the fourth tool down on the right side).

2. Click, hold, and drag your mouse around a small area. You will see that you are painting color onto your image.

   If your Brush is too small or too large, you can use the Options bar to choose a different-size brush. Click on the pop-up menu noted by a small downward-pointing triangle to see a box filled with different brush sizes. Some are hard-edged, some are soft-edged. In the lower portion of the box are interesting shapes that can also be used as brushes. (In older versions of Photoshop, the brushes are available from a Brushes palette rather than in the Options bar.)

   Choose a brush size and type. Pick a different foreground color and paint a small swatch of color right next to your first color swatch.

   Your goal is to find colors that look good next to each other. This is a good way to determine which colors you would like to use for the backgrounds, buttons, logos, and other images on your Web site.

Harmonious Color Schemes

When you are choosing colors, here are some ideas for picking *harmonious color schemes*—colors that work well together:

☆ *Analogous colors* are colors that are similar, for example, blue, purple, and lavender.

☆ *Monochromatic colors* are colors that are from the same family, for example, dark blue, medium blue, and light blue.

☆ *Complementary colors* are colors that are not from the same family, for example, purple and yellow, red and green.

☆ *Neutral colors* are ones in which color appears diminished, for example, gray, beige, and khaki.

Continue to create the color guide by painting colors on your image. Try to find five or six colors that look good next to each other. You may wish to create more

Using the Painting Tools to Make a Color Guide

than one color guide, each expressing a different *mood* or *personality* for a Web site. Figure 1.7 shows an example of a color guide that uses bright complementary colors—ones that might appeal to children.

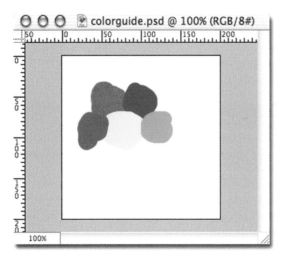

Figure 1.7 Color Guide

Tools and Techniques for Choosing and Saving Colors

Use the tools and techniques explained here to help you choose and save colors.

Using the Eyedropper Tool

If you wish to go back to a color you've already painted on your image, but you forget exactly which color it is, use Photoshop's Eyedropper tool. The Eyedropper is the second to last tool in the Toolbox on the right side above the color chips. It gives you another way to pick colors.

Choose the Eyedropper tool and then click one of the colors in your image. You will see that the color now becomes the active color in the Foreground box in the Toolbox and in the Color palette.

You can pick colors with the Eyedropper tool from anywhere on the screen, including any other open image.

Using the Color Picker Spectrum to Create a Color Guide

Here is a simple way to choose a harmonious color scheme.

1. Click on the Foreground color box in the Toolbox to open the Color Picker. In the large square to the left you will see a small circle that identifies the currently active Foreground color. If it is not already chosen, click a color that will be the main color in your color scheme.

2. The column down the middle of the Color Picker contains a **spectrum**, or range of colors.

3. Click and hold on one of the arrows next to the spectrum. Drag your mouse to move the arrow up and down the spectrum. When you stop the arrow, the colors in the box on the left will change. The small circle will identify a color that contains the same *values*, or *lightness/darkness*, of your active color. This is a good way to pick colors that are analogous, monochromatic, complementary, or neutral and that also *match in value*. Choose a color and click OK.

4. This new color will become the active Foreground color. Paint this color next to your previous color on your image. Go back to the Color Picker and choose another matching color. Paint it on your image. Repeat this exercise until you have five or six colors that look good next to each other.

5. You've created a **color guide**. You have a set of colors, or a palette, that identifies the harmonious color scheme you will use for your Web site.

Saving the Colors in Your Color Guide

You can save your colors so that they will be easy to identify the next time you are working on an image. In the bottom row of the Swatches palette, there are some empty spaces where no colors appear.

1. Use the Eyedropper tool to pick one of the colors in your color guide.

2. Move your mouse to one of the empty areas of the Swatches palette. The pointer will change from an eyedropper to a paint bucket.

3. Click in one of the empty areas. A box will appear, allowing you to name the color swatch. Name it, click OK, and your color will be added to the Swatches palette.

4. Repeat this with each of the colors in your color guide. You may wish to use names that relate to the specific project you are working on.

5. The colors will be saved in the Swatches palette when you close the program, and you can reuse them later for another project.

You can also remember your colors from one time to the next by writing down the hexadecimal or RGB codes that appear in the Color palette. (See "Style Guide" in Chapter Eight for more information.)

◎◎ Saving Your Images in the Correct Format for the Web

You can create many different types, or **formats**, of images on a computer. Some image formats are used specifically for printing. Some are used exclusively by the program that created them. Some are used just for animations. Some are used for more than one purpose.

Photoshop has its own format built into the program. It is called **PSD**. It is an important image format because it includes special features available only in the Photoshop program. To take advantage of these special features, you must save your image in the PSD format. You'll learn more about these features in the chapters that follow. When you create an original image, you should save it in the PSD format so that you can edit it later.

You will also save a copy of the image in a format suited for the Web for use on your Web site. PSD images may not be used on the Web.

There are two primary image formats that are used for the Web: (1) **GIF** images (pronounced with a hard *g* or a soft *g*—either is correct) and (2) **JPG** (pronounced *jay-peg*) images.

PNG is another image format that is becoming popular for use on the Web. You will not work with PNG images in this book.

Each of these image formats has a specific purpose. When you save your image for the Web, you should use an appropriate format.

The **GIF format** is used for images that contain blocks of solid colors. It is used primarily for images that are considered *graphics*. They contain shapes and/or text. The shapes or text consist of hard-edged lines, often placed on a background of solid color. The color guide image you just created is a good example of an image that should be saved in the GIF format.

The **JPG format** is used for images that contain shadings or gradations of colors. It is the best format for photographs and images that contain many subtle blends of color. If you scan a photograph you've taken with a regular camera, you should probably save the image in the JPG format. Most images acquired from digital cameras are already produced in the JPG format.

Save Menu Commands

The File menu contains three commands that you use to save images. Each has a specific purpose:

☆ **Save**: Use this command the first time you save your image and each time after that when you wish to save the image exactly as it is.

☆ **Save As**: Use this command when you want to save a copy of your image in another location and/or with a different name.

☆ **Save for Web**: Use this command when you want to save a copy of your image in either the GIF or the JPG format for your Web site.

You'll learn *how* to use those commands in just a bit, but first, you should understand *why* you use them.

Guidelines for Saving and Naming Images

When you create an image by using the New command in the File menu, a blank image appears on the desktop. It has the generic name Untitled. If you create several new images, they will be successively numbered. They will have names like *Untitled-1*, *Untitled-2*, and so on.

Naming Images and Folders

As soon as you create a new image, you should save it. The way you name your image and the format in which you save it are important. By following the guidelines listed here, you will be sure that your images will be compatible with documents and software used in creating editable images and images for use on Web sites.

☆ Give your image a name that consists of lowercase letters. Sometimes you can use a capital letter to create a distinction between two words. For example: colorGuide.psd.

☆ Make the name as brief as possible.

☆ Do not use any of the special characters on your keyboard, such as the asterisk, percent sign, comma, period, apostrophe, or slash.

☆ Do not include any spaces in the name of your image.

☆ Names for folders do not always have to be quite so restricted as image names, but it is a good idea to keep folder names as short and simple as possible, too. Unless you are sure about what you are doing, use the same naming guidelines for folders as for images.

Each image you create and save will be processed in a particular format, depending on how you saved the image.

☆**WARNING** Naming Your Images

This book capitalizes GIF, JPG, and PSD to make them easily recognizable in the text. But when you name your images, you should always use lowercase letters.

Strategy for Saving Your Images

In no time at all, you will have dozens of images. Keeping them sorted with particular folder location and file-naming strategies is important.

1. Keep a folder called *Master Originals* where you store all your original images. If you have scanned them, they should be saved as PSD images. If they came from a digital camera, they will probably be JPG images. If they came from a clip art or photo compilation CD, they will use a format determined by the CD publisher. If you saved them from a Web site, they will probably be GIF, JPG, or PNG files. In all cases, these should be the original images you acquired. Do not edit these images.

2. For each project you work on, create a folder for the materials you will use. Use copies of your Master Original images to edit for the specific project. These *copies* will be your *Project* images. You should save these copies in the PSD format so that you can use the special features of Photoshop to edit them.

3. When you are ready to create an image to be used on a Web site, you will create yet another copy of the image. It will be saved in the appropriate format

(GIF or JPG) in an appropriate folder. You can refer to this file as your *Output* image. At the end of this chapter you will learn to save an image in the GIF format.

Earlier in this chapter, you used Photoshop to create an image that includes the color guide you will use for your Web site. When you save that image for the first time, you should save it in the PSD format and put it in your Master Originals folder. Then create a copy of the image and place it in your Project folder. Edit that *copy* of the image, not the original. An example follows.

1. The file colorGuide.psd is the file you created. Save it in your Master Originals folder.

2. Now *save a copy of it* in the PSD format in your Project folder. Use this image for editing.

3. When you are ready to put the image on your Web site, *save another copy* (of the edited Project image) in the GIF format. Name this file colorguide.gif. It is your *Output* image. Put it in a folder called *images*.

4. See the end of this chapter for information on how to save a GIF file.

You cannot use Photoshop's special features with an image when it is in the GIF format, so you should not edit your GIF image. Your GIF image is for the Web only.

If you ever want to go back and use Photoshop's special editing features to edit your image, use the PSD image from your Project folder.

Meanwhile, your original image will reside in the Master Originals folder, where you can retrieve a copy of it should you lose or ruin your Project file. You can also make a copy of the master image for another new project.

The activities and exercises in this book assume that you have saved a Master Original copy of your image and that you are working on a copy from your Project folder.

Using the Three Save Commands

The following procedures explain how to use the three different Save commands that are available in the File menu.

Using the Save Command

When you save your image for the first time, go to the File Menu and choose Save. For the location, choose the folder you've created for your Master Original images. Name your image according to the naming guidelines already mentioned. Be sure the Format is Photoshop. Click the Save button.

The file name of every image you save should automatically include an **extension** that identifies the file type. The complete name of your image includes the name you gave it, followed by a period (.) and a three-letter extension, or abbreviation, which indicates the format of the image. (Remember that PSD, GIF, and JPG are image formats.)

In Windows computers, you may not see the .PSD extension at the end of the file name, but you will see the word "Photoshop" in the Format pop-up box. If "Photoshop" is not selected, use the pop-up menu to select it.

In Mac computers, you should see the .PSD extension added to your image name. If you don't see it, type it after the image name. Make sure "Photoshop" is chosen in the Format pop-up box.

When you save an image in the Photoshop (PSD) format, Photoshop's special editing features will be available to you. As you proceed through this book, you will learn more about the features that are only available to an image saved in the PSD format.

☆ **WARNING**   **Keeping Track of Extensions**

On many computers, file extensions are turned *off* by default. This means that you do not see the file extension in the name of an image. As a novice Web designer, you may want to turn *on* the display of file extensions by using the preference settings in your computer. This way you will be better able to keep track of the various types of files you save when creating images for the Web.

Using the Save As Command

Use the Save As command to make a *copy* of an image for your Project folder. Do this whenever you are starting a new project and want to use a copy of one of the images from your Master Originals folder.

Also, there are times when you may want to save a copy of your image with another image name. For example, you might want to experiment with different colors or text on a different copy of the image. Use the File Menu to choose Save As, and give your image another name, for example, colorGuide2.psd.

Be sure that the Format pop-up box indicates Photoshop as the format. There are many other formats listed in the pop-up box, but most relate to images for print or other advanced techniques that are not covered in this book.

Using the Save for Web Command

When you are ready to save a copy of your image for your Web site, go to the File menu and choose the Save for Web command. A box will open that looks very different from the Save and Save As boxes.

The Save for Web box lets you choose either the GIF or the JPG format, which are appropriate formats for the Web. You also use this box to make particular settings that **optimize**, or fine-tune, your image so that it will look its best and download quickly from a Web browser. As you read the next section, refer to Figure 1.8, which shows the Save for Web box.

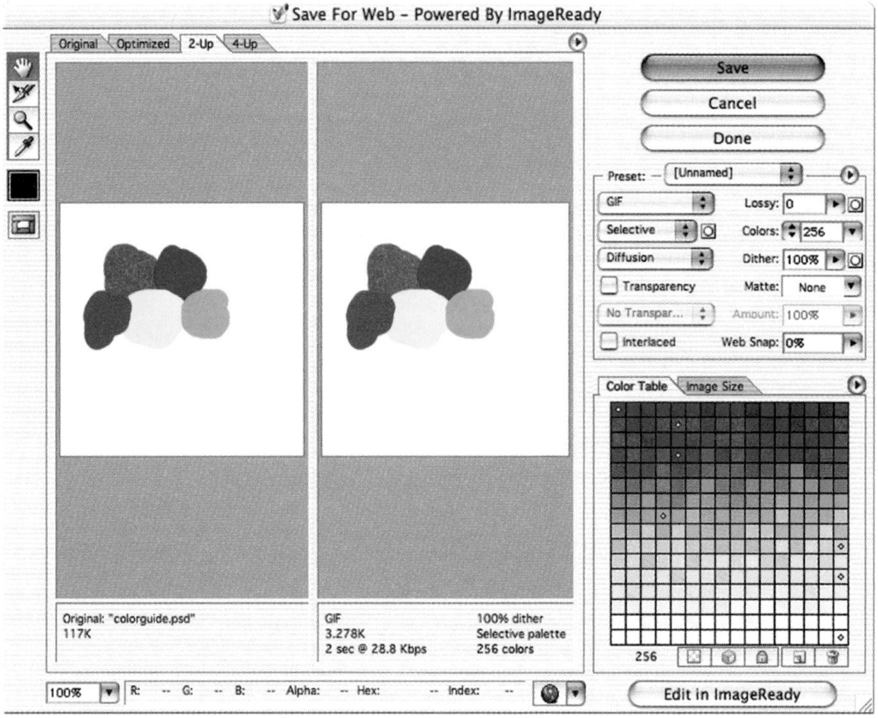

Figure 1.8 Save for Web Box

The four tabs across the top of the Save for Web box at the left are as follows:

☆ **Original** shows your image as you created it in Photoshop. In Figure 1.8, the original image appears in the large area that takes up the left one-third of the Save for Web box.

☆ **Optimized** shows your image as it will appear if you use the particular settings that appear on the right side of the Save for Web box.

☆ **2-up** gives you a split-pane view. It shows your original image on the left and the optimized image on the right.

☆ **4-up** shows you another split-pane view. Your original image is at the top left. The other three views show you optimized images based on three different groups of settings. Thus you can experiment with different settings, so you can choose to save whichever image works best for you.

The tools at the far left of the Save for Web box are as follows:

☆ **Hand** lets you move the image around in the boxes.

☆ **Slice Select** lets you choose particular slices of your image. You will learn how to use slices in Chapter Seven.

☆ **Zoom** lets you click a portion of your image to magnify it.

☆ **Eyedropper**, an eyedropper color box, and a button to toggle among selected slices are also available here. You do not have to be concerned about these tools now.

Saving a GIF Image for the Web

The following procedures explain how to save a GIF image for the Web.

1. Choose the 2-up tab at the top of the Save for Web box. Choose the Hand tool in the far left column. Now click each of the two views of your image. When you click one of the views, it becomes the active view and appears to have a darker border around the box it is in.

2. Click on the view that is not your original image. At the bottom of the box you will see a summary of the settings that are selected on the right. Also indicated is the **size**, in kilobytes, of your image, and the amount of time it will take to download this image from the Web if you are using a modem. Your goal is to produce an image that is small in size, downloads quickly, yet looks as good as possible. See "File Size" in Chapter Eight for more information.

3. At the right side of the Save for Web box, there are two columns of boxes and settings. At the top of the left column is a pop-up box where you can choose GIF or JPG, the two image formats for the Web. Choose GIF. In Chapters Two and Three, you will learn more about other settings in the Save for Web box.

4. When you are ready, click OK. Choose a location for your image. For example, put it in a folder you create for your Web images, probably named *images*. The GIF extension should already be added for you. Click Save.

☆ **WARNING** Saving the Correct Format

Using the Save for Web command is an important step in creating an image for a Web site. When you choose the GIF (or JPG) format and save the image, the correct processing will take place to make the image an actual GIF (or JPG) file. You cannot force an image to contain the correct format simply by naming or renaming it. It must be *processed* in the correct format using the Save for Web command.

You've created a Photoshop image and saved it in the GIF format for your Web site. In Chapter Two you will learn how to save a digital or scanned photograph in the JPG image format. In subsequent chapters, you will learn more details about the Save for Web box.

☆ Summary

▷ Photoshop allows you to create and edit images, place images on top of each other in layers, and create animations and Web pages.

▷ The work area contains tools and boxes that you use to edit your images. You can move tools and boxes around to customize them for the way you work.

▷ Color is a complicated subject but an important one for image making. There are special color modes for viewing images on a computer monitor.

▷ Using Photoshop's color tools, you can select a color scheme for your images and Web site.

▷ The GIF format is used for images that contain solid blocks of color and/or hard edges like text and graphics against a background color.

☆ Online References

The Adobe Web site. Explore the site and find a variety of useful information about Photoshop and other Adobe products.
http://www.adobe.com

Color Theory from Brown University
http://www.cs.brown.edu/courses/cs092/VA10/HTML/start.html

Visibone—the Webmaster's Color Laboratory
http://www.visibone.com/colorlab

ColorMatters—a great collection of information about color
http://www.colormatters.com/colortheory.html

The Kodak Digital Learning Center—Color Theory
http://www.kodak.com/US/en/digital/dlc/book3/chapter2/index.shtml

A collection of products, resources, and tips related to imagery
http://www.eyewire.com

More than you would ever want to know about the GIF format
http://256.com/gray/docs/gifspecs/

☆ Review Questions

1. Name six ways to create an image in Photoshop.

2. How did the Web 216 color palette come to be used by Web designers? Why is it not so widely used today?

3. What are the three color modes used most in Web design?

4. What is the importance of making a color guide?

5. What are the advantages of developing a saving strategy like the one proposed here? What is the Master Originals folder used for? What is the Project folder used for? What are Output files like GIFs and JPGs used for?

6. When is it appropriate to save an image in the GIF format? In the JPG format?

7. What colors might you use for a children's Web site? For a bank's Web site? For a landscaping company's Web site? For a race car Web site?

☆ Hands-On Exercises

If you have access to the companion Web site for this book, use those files for the exercises.

1. The grayscale test is always a good way to test your colors to see if you have good contrast on your Web page. Choose two colors and paint one color next to the other. In the Image→Mode menu, choose Grayscale. Notice the color values, or contrast between the two colors. Would this be a good choice for display on your Web site? Try several different color combinations to see what combinations have the best contrast.

2. Create two color guides, one for a children's Web site and one for a Fortune 500 financial company. Compare the sets of colors you have chosen, and explain your color choices.

3. Create two more color guides, one for a trendy nightspot and one for a yoga training class. Compare the sets of colors you have chosen, and explain your color choices.

4. Create two more color guides, one using the Web 216 color palette and one using all available RGB colors. Explain the differences you encountered in each process. Show these color guides to others and ask for their feedback.

5. Develop your saving strategy. Create a folder for your Master Originals, one for your Project images, and one for your Output, or GIF, images. Save some images into each folder in the correct format.

CHAPTER TWO

ACQUIRING AND EDITING IMAGES

One of the most common reasons to use Photoshop is to work with an already existing image. You may have photos you've taken with your digital or film camera that you want to put on your Web site. Photoshop can work directly with your scanner to acquire an image and can open existing digital images. Photoshop includes an amazing array of tools for editing your images and optimizing them for the Web.

Chapter Objectives

☆ Use the best practices for scanning a photograph, drawing, or object

☆ Use basic tools in Photoshop to edit your image

☆ Learn about image size and resolution

☆ Learn some common image sizes for the Web

☆ Use tools in Photoshop to create interesting effects

☆ Save your image in the JPG format

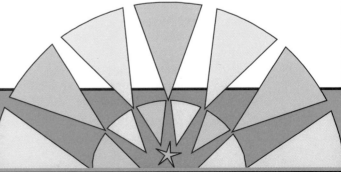

◎◎ Scanning

A scanner works very much like an office copying machine. You place your document or photograph face down on the glass, click to select certain settings, and a copy of the image appears on your computer screen.

When you buy a scanner, it comes with its own software that is required for the scanning process. If your scanner is compatible with Photoshop and if you have Photoshop already installed on your computer at the time you install the scanning software, a small piece of software called a driver automatically becomes available within your Photoshop software.

☆ **WARNING** **About Scanners and Drivers**

If your scanner is not compatible with Photoshop, you may have to scan your photograph using the scanner's software and then open the resulting image in Photoshop separately. For assistance with determining the correct driver for use with Photoshop, consult the documentation that came with your scanner.

The driver allows you to begin your scan in Photoshop. When you are ready to scan, go to Photoshop's File menu and choose Import. A box will pop up that includes a list of scanning methods. The name of the driver that goes with your scanner should appear in the list. Click to select the driver.

At this point, the processing software that your scanner uses will appear. There are many types of scanners and scanner software, so this book does not review the exact details for your particular scanner.

General Principles for Scanning

Many scanners come with Easy and Advanced interfaces. If you choose Easy, your scanning experience will be exactly that. The downside is that you are not really aware of the details regarding the acquisition of your image. Sometimes an Easy scan does not result in an image that is the best it can be for your purposes. As a Web designer, you should learn the concepts involved in an Advanced scan.

1. Scan your photo at a resolution of 150 dots per inch (dpi), even though you will lower the resolution later when you save a copy of your image for the Web. (You will learn more about resolution in this chapter.)

2. If you want to enlarge the physical dimensions of your photo for placement on the Web, make the enlargement settings at the time you do the scan. If you enlarge it later using Photoshop or other techniques, you may degrade the quality of your image.

3. If you are scanning a color photo, use the highest possible color settings at the time you do the scan. For example, use True Color or Millions of Colors.

4. If you are scanning an image from a newspaper or magazine, be sure to use the option called Descreen. Using a Descreen setting will result in a clear

image. If you do not use this setting, your image may appear to have what is called a moiré pattern, a series of dots or boxes that muddy your image.

5. Usually, you can crop and rotate your image within the interface of the scanning software. You can also do these tasks in Photoshop.

In Figure 2.1a, the original image was half the size shown. It was scanned at 200% to fit the requirements of the user's Web site. In Figure 2.1b, the same image was scanned at its actual size and enlarged later in Photoshop. You can also enlarge images with HTML code. Neither of these methods results in a high-quality image because the same pixels from the smaller image are used to create the new dimensions of the enlarged image. Scanning with a larger scale setting packs additional pixels into the image, thus creating a higher-quality image.

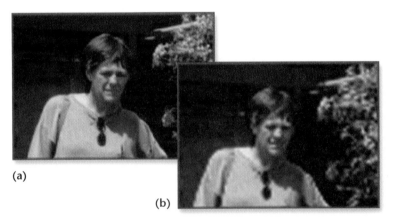

(a)

(b)

Figure 2.1 (a) Image Scanned at 200% (b) Same Image Scanned at 100% and Enlarged Later in Photoshop

Do-overs are inevitable. Sometimes you will have to scan an image more than once to be sure you have the best possible image. You may scan an image with particular settings only to realize later that you need to enlarge the image. If so, go back and scan it again with different settings.

Ways to Acquire Images Besides Scanning

Scanning is not the only way to acquire an image. Following are other ways you might acquire an image for use in Photoshop.

☆ You can acquire a photograph from a digital camera. Use the directions and software that came with your camera to download the images into your computer.

☆ You can acquire images by using clip art or stock photography. Certain Web sites allow you to download free clip art and photos. You can also purchase artwork and photos from Web sites or on compilation CD-ROMs.

☆ You can use your computer to take a picture of something on your monitor. In Windows, press the Print Screen key at the top of your keyboard. A picture of whatever is showing on your monitor will be saved in the computer's "clipboard" memory. Then open Photoshop, create a New File, and Paste the saved picture. On a Mac, use the ⌘-Shift-3 or ⌘-Shift-4 keystroke combinations to either capture the entire screen area or to select a portion of the screen. The resulting images will be saved to your hard drive or desktop. Open them in Photoshop to edit.

☆ You can create your own original images. See Chapter Three for information on creating your own logos, icons, buttons, and images.

☆ Keep your original digital photos, your original scans, and your originals acquired from other sources in your Master Originals folder. Do not edit them. Use Save As to create a copy in your Project folder and edit the copy.

⌾⌾ Editing an Image: The Basic Tools

There are many tools in Photoshop that allow you to edit images. In this chapter you will learn some of the basic tools. First, be sure to save your image.

Saving a Scanned Image

Once your scan is completed, the scanning software interface will close, and your image will appear in the Photoshop work area. You should save your image as soon as possible. Go to the File menu and choose Save. As you learned in Chapter One, give the image a brief, lowercase name and be sure the Format is set to "Photoshop." Save the image into your *Master Originals* folder.

Saving a Copy of an Image

Whether you have scanned an image or acquired one from a digital camera or other source, you should save your original in your Master Originals folder. Then make a copy of the image for editing for a particular project.

1. Assuming you have already saved the scanned or other image to your Master Originals folder and the image is still open in Photoshop, choose Save As from the File menu.

2. In the box that appears, click the checkbox next to As a Copy. Photoshop will automatically put the word "copy" in the name of the image.

3. In the Format pop-up box, choose "Photoshop."

4. Set the Save As location to your *Project* folder and click Save. A copy of your image will be saved.

5. The Photoshop work area will still contain the original image you saved to your Master Originals folder. Close the image by choosing File→Close.

6. Choose File→Open to open the copy of the image that is in your Project folder. Now you can edit the copy of the image without affecting your Master Original.

Now you are ready to make some basic image-editing modifications that will result in the best possible image for your Web site.

For the activities in the rest of this chapter, be sure you are working on a copy of your image. If you followed the guidelines in step 2, the name of your image will contain the word "copy," and it will be easy to see if you are working on the correct image.

Rotating the Canvas

Sometimes when you scan a photo, you realize that you accidentally put it on the scanner upside down or sideways. Maybe you did it on purpose because it was the only way it would fit on the scanner. Sometimes a photo from a digital camera is oriented sideways.

To reorient the image, go to the Image menu and choose Rotate Canvas. In the pop-up box that appears, choose the degrees and direction necessary to place the image correctly. You can also use this menu to flip your image horizontally or vertically. Be careful of flipping images that have text in them because the text may read backwards after the image is flipped.

Cropping an Image

Most photographs that are developed from film cameras are sized at 3½ by 5 inches or 4 by 6 inches. In most cases, these sizes are too large for a Web page.

For the typical Web site, medium and small images are best. A large image takes longer to download, frustrating users of your Web site. But if you simply make the entire image smaller, you run the risk that the important parts of the image become too small to see.

Often only a part of the image is the portion you wish to focus on, and the rest is distracting and unnecessary—especially for the Web. The best solution to these problems may be cropping the image.

Sometimes it is hard for novices to decide to crop a photograph. They want viewers to see the entire photo. But because large photos are often not appropriate for Web sites, you should learn to look very closely at photos to determine the most important areas. By cropping to show only the important areas, you will be sure that your image is large enough to have impact.

Photoshop contains a very useful tool for cropping, the Crop tool.

☆ **WARNING** **Finding the Crop Tool**

In Photoshop 6.0 and later versions, the **Crop tool** is the third tool down in the left column of the Toolbox. In earlier versions, the Crop tool is bundled in with the Marquee tool at the top of the left column. You have to click the selection tool and drag out to choose the Crop tool.

Following are some steps for using the Crop tool.

1. Select the Crop tool in the Toolbox.

2. Move your mouse to the area of the photograph you would like to keep.

3. You will see that the pointer has changed into an icon of the Crop tool.

4. Click, hold, and drag your mouse to create a box around part of the image.

5. Let go of the mouse.

6. You will see that a moving, dashed line, sometimes called **marching ants**, surrounds the part of the image you selected. You will also notice that there are small boxes at the corners of the selection box and at the midpoints of each side. You can drag the small boxes in or out to resize the selection box.

7. If you drag the corner boxes, you resize the whole selection. If you drag one of the middle boxes, you resize only that side of the selection box.

8. When you've selected the portion of the image you want to keep, go to the Image menu and choose Crop. The part of the image outside your selection box will disappear and your image will be cropped.

☆**TIP**   **Straightening an Image with the Crop Tool**

The Crop tool can also be used to straighten the horizontal plane of an image with a crooked horizon line. Select the Crop tool and drag a selection around the image. Place your mouse above one of the corners until it turns into a curved arrow. Click, hold, and drag until the selection box matches the plane in the photo. Then choose Crop in the Image menu.

Photoshop CS and later versions include an automatic function to crop and straighten a photo. From the File menu, choose Automate→Crop and Straighten Photos. The procedure will be performed automatically.

Adjusting Black and White Levels

Lighting conditions are very important when you are taking photographs. If you are not a professional photographer, you probably have several photos that appear washed out or too dark because the lighting was not ideal.

After you scan one of these photos, you can adjust the levels of black and white in your scanned image. Go to the Image menu and choose Adjustments. Then choose Auto Levels. You will see the effect on your image. Photoshop automatically calculates the amount of black and white that need to be added to or subtracted from your image to correct it. Figure 2.2 shows a poorly lit photograph that was corrected with Auto Levels.

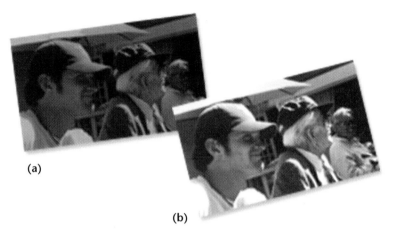

(a)

(b)

Figure 2.2 (a) Image Taken in Poor Lighting Conditions (b) Same Image with Auto Levels Applied

Sometimes you will not be satisfied with the automatic adjustment that Photoshop makes. To make the black and white adjustment manually, go to the Image menu and choose Adjustments. Then choose Levels. You will see what is called a **histogram**, which represents the amount of colors in your image. Use the sliders in the histogram to make the adjustment.

1. In the center of the box, if you drag one of the upward-pointed arrows on each end of the histogram, you can change the amount of black and white in your image.

2. When you drag the left side in toward the center, you are adding black.

3. When you drag the right side in toward the center, you are adding white.

You can also automatically adjust the Contrast of your image by choosing Auto Contrast in the Image→Adjust menu. Or you can choose Brightness/Contrast to make the adjustments manually. Experiment until you are comfortable using these tools.

Many nuances and complexities are involved in using the Levels histogram and the other contrast tools. When you become more experienced, you can use Photoshop's Help menu to learn more.

Adjusting the Colors

Maybe you have a photo that has great potential, but the colors appear to be washed out, and you would like to punch them up a bit. Maybe you would like to "colorize" your photo by replacing all the colors with one hue. Both techniques are interesting ways to enhance your images.

You can use the Image→Adjust→Hue/Saturation menu to make these types of changes.

In the Hue/Saturation box, move the Saturation slider to increase the saturation. Notice the effect on the colors in your image.

If you wish to tint your photo, click the checkbox in the lower right labeled Colorize. The actual colors will be removed from your image. Then move the Hue slider back and forth to find a hue that you like.

Figure 2.3 shows three images. Figure 2.3c is an image that has been colorized with the Hue/Saturation box for dramatic effect. Figure 2.3a is a photograph that was taken with incorrect settings and appears washed out. In Figure 2.3b, the same image appears more brilliant because increased saturation was applied in the Hue/Saturation box.

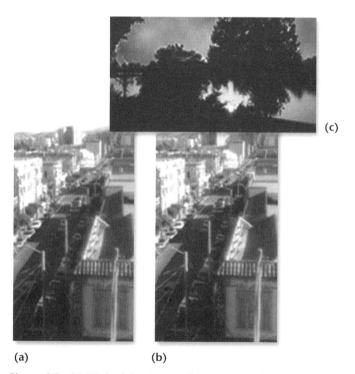

(c)

(a)   (b)

Figure 2.3   (a) Washed-Out Image (b) Image to Which Increased Saturation Has Been Applied (c) Image Colorized with a Tint

Advanced users of Photoshop will find many other tools, such as Curves, Color Balance, and Color Replacement, for changing and correcting colors in an image. As you become more experienced, you can use Photoshop's Help menu to learn more about these specialized options.

Sharpening the Image

When you scan a photograph, you will often lose a bit of sharpness around the edges. Sometimes your photo was a bit blurry to begin with. It's usually a good idea to use the Unsharp Mask filter after you scan to sharpen up the photo.

1. Go to the Filter menu, choose Sharpen, and choose Unsharp Mask.

2. A box appears with a small preview window and Amount, Radius, and Threshold settings. Type a number in the Amount box. Notice the effect on your image. (For novice designers, it is probably best to leave the Radius setting at 1 pixel and the Threshold setting at 0 levels.)

3. As a matter of routine, you should probably apply Unsharp Mask to all your scanned photos, using an Amount of somewhere between 20% and 50%.

4. If you apply Unsharp Mask but are not satisfied with the result, choose Edit→Undo. Then, go back and choose different settings until you are satisfied. Using too much Unsharp Mask can make your image look too digital and less realistic.

☆ **WARNING** Use the Unsharp Mask Filter Last

If you are making several changes—or edits—to your image, use the Unsharp Mask filter last. In general, avoid using the other sharpening tools that are available in the Sharpen filter pop-up menu. Only advanced users should use those tools.

◎◎ Image Size and Resolution

Before you go on to use other editing tools in Photoshop, you should learn more about pixels, image size, and resolution. These concepts are important to the quality of your image, and are important to the way the image appears on your Web site.

☆ **SHORTCUT** Turning Rulers On and Off

You should turn Rulers on so that you can begin to become comfortable with pixels as a unit of measurement. You can easily toggle Rulers on and off by using the keyboard shortcut Control-R (Windows) or ⌘-R (Mac). Set the Preferences in Photoshop to use pixels as the unit of measurement.

What Is a Pixel?

A **pixel** is a tiny square that is the smallest unit of measurement for television screens and computer monitors. There are about 72 pixels in every square inch of your screen or monitor. This is different from printed material where there can be many thousands of units in every inch, making extremely high-quality printed images possible.

When you scanned your image, you set the Resolution to 150 dots per inch, or dpi, a printer's term. As Web designers, we say pixels per inch rather than dots per inch, but these terms mean the same thing—every inch of an image is composed of hundreds or thousands of tiny pixels or dots.

An image composed of 150 dpi is generally a higher-quality image than one composed of 72 dpi. The more dots or pixels filled with colors, shapes, or parts of the image, the higher the quality of the image.

Most scanning software uses the term dpi or dots per inch. But when you are working in Photoshop to prepare an image for the Web, you will use pixels per inch, or ppi.

Rationale for the Saving Strategy

Remember that you should scan your images at a minimum of 150 dpi—or pixels per inch. By doing so and saving the image in your Master Originals folder, you will always have a high-quality version of the image available. It may be that you will want to print an image for use as a flyer or CD cover. If so, your master original at 150 dpi will assure good printing quality.

After you save a copy of the image in your Project folder, you should lower the dpi to 72 in the Image Size box. In doing so, you will be preparing the image for output as a Web image.

☆**TIP**   **How Many Pixels Do You Need?**

As a general rule of thumb, the resolution of images for display on a Web site should be 72 pixels per inch. If you are going to print an image on your desktop printer, you should use images composed of at least 150 pixels per inch. If you wish to print your images in a magazine or color brochure, you should use at least 300 pixels per inch. For extremely high-quality printing, you would use even more pixels per inch.

The study of pixels and computer monitors can be a complicated subject. To keep things simple, most designers use 72 pixels per inch as a general guide for Web images.

Using the Image Size Box

Figure 2.4 shows the Image Size box. The top area of the box is labeled Pixel Dimensions and shows the width and height of your image in pixels. The lower area of the box is labeled Document Size; it shows the width and height of your image in inches. The lower area of the box also shows the Resolution, or the number of pixels in each inch of your image.

To change the image size, follow these steps.

1. Check to be sure that you are working on a copy of your image from the Projects folder.

2. Go to the Image menu and choose Image Size.

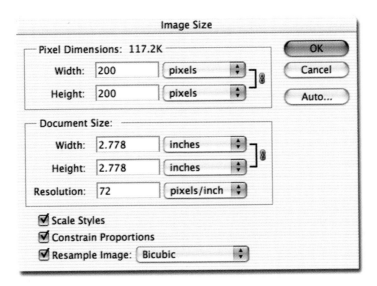

Figure 2.4 Image Size Box

3. At the bottom of the box are two checkable boxes labeled Constrain Proportions and Resample Image. Make sure both boxes are checked.

4. Because you will put this image on your Web site, you should change the resolution to 72 pixels per inch. In the box labeled Resolution, delete the 150 and type 72. Notice that the Pixel Dimensions automatically change. When you reduced the number of pixels per inch, you automatically reduced the total number of pixels making up the image.

5. When the Resample Image box is checked and you change the size of your image, Photoshop correspondingly adjusts the total number of pixels in the image. If you do not check the Resample Image box, the total number of pixels remains the same, even if you resize the image's dimensions in inches. For images used on the Web, it is probably best to keep the Resample Image box checked so that the final file size is as small as possible and will download quickly.

6. When the Constrain Proportions box is checked and you make a change to one dimension of your image, the other dimension automatically changes.

7. Photoshop CS and later versions include a checkbox titled Scale Styles. Novices should leave this box checked.

In Figure 2.5, the image has been distorted because only one dimension was changed. Check the Constrain Proportions box in the Image Size box to prevent this from happening. For example, if you have an image that is 4 inches wide and 6 inches high and you change the width to 6 inches without changing the height, the image will appear stretched. The Constrain Proportions box prevents this from happening by automatically changing the height proportionally after you've made a change to the width or vice versa.

Figure 2.5 Distorted Image

Relationship Between Pixels, Image Size, and Resolution

You can make changes to the size of your image by typing numbers into the boxes in the Pixel Dimensions and/or the Document Size area in the Image Size box.

Although most of us are familiar with measurements in inches, as a Web designer it is a good idea to be comfortable with pixels as your unit of measurement.

1. Choose Image→Image Size from the Menu bar. In the box that appears, be sure the Resample Image box is checked. Set the Resolution to 72.

2. To help you get a sense of pixels versus inches, you can use some familiar numbers. Type 8.5 for the width in inches in the Document Size area. Type 11 for the height in inches in the same area.

3. Notice that the pixel dimensions at the top of the box have automatically changed. The dimensions of a standard sheet of paper are 8½ inches by 11 inches so you have some idea of the size you are dealing with.

4. 8½ inches is the same as 612 pixels (8.5 inches × 72 pixels per inch = 612 pixels).

5. 11 inches is the same as 792 pixels (11 inches × 72 pixels per inch = 792 pixels).

The number of pixels in the width and height of your image is directly related to both the Resolution of your image and the actual physical size of your image.

☆ If you change the resolution of your image, you automatically change the number of pixels in the actual size of your image (assuming that the Resample Image box is checked).

☆ After you set the resolution in the Image Size box, you can change the pixel dimensions to further change the actual size of your image.

Monitor Resolution and the Web

Computer monitors are produced with fixed sizes, such as a 15-inch monitor, 17-inch monitor, 19-inch monitor, and so on. Computer monitors use the term **resolution** to refer not only to the 72-pixels-per-inch definition, presented in the preceding section, but also to the minimum and maximum widths of information displayed on the monitor.

Not too long ago, computer monitors were capable of displaying a monitor resolution of only 640 pixels wide by 480 pixels high. If you produce an image with exactly those pixel dimensions, your image will fill the screen on one of those monitors.

Modern computer monitors are capable of displaying multiple monitor resolutions, some as high as 1920 pixels wide by 1080 pixels high. As a Web designer, you are challenged because you do not know which resolution users have on their monitors.

As of the date of this publication, most computer users are using a monitor resolution of at least 800 pixels wide by 600 pixels high. As a Web designer, you can use this information to help determine what size your Web pages and Web images should be. You will learn more about monitor resolution, Web page sizes, and Web images in Chapter Six.

Common Image Sizes for the Web

If you produce an image that is the size of a standard sheet of paper, 612 pixels wide by 792 pixels high, your image will extend to about two thirds of the width of a Web page sized for an 800-pixel-wide monitor. To see the bottom of the image, users would have to scroll down. An image this size is probably too large for a Web page. Not only would there be little room left for other information, but the image would take a very long time to download, frustrating users of your Web site.

Following are some common image sizes:

☆ If you have a photograph to put on your Web page, you should probably crop and/or size it to a maximum width of 200 or 300 pixels.

☆ Small icons are usually around 50 pixels wide and high.

☆ Buttons are usually around 100 pixels wide and 50 pixels high.

There are no "right" sizes; you have to decide what works for your Web page. There is always a trade-off in making images that are large enough to be compelling yet small enough to download quickly. See "File Size" in Chapter Eight for more information.

☆**TIP**   **Image Size and Digital Photographs**

If you open a photograph taken from a digital camera in Photoshop, the resolution may be 72 pixels per inch, but the pixel dimensions may be very large—perhaps thousands of pixels wide and high.

You will have to decrease the pixel dimensions to make this image fit on your Web page. Be sure you are working on a copy of your image. Choose Image→Image Size from the Menu bar to make the changes in the Pixel Dimensions boxes.

Image Size and Resolution

◎◎ Editing Your Image: Fun with Photoshop

Now that you know what size to make your image, you can learn to use other Photoshop tools to make your image more compelling. Scan a photograph at 150 dpi, or download a photo from your digital camera, and save it to your Master Originals folder.

Save a copy of the photo in your Projects folder and use the copy for the following activities. Crop the photo if you wish. Open the Image→Image Size box and set the resolution at 72. If you want to reduce the physical size of your image, enter new pixel dimensions for the width and height.

Using Filters

Click the Filter menu and notice the list of items. Choose one of the items and notice the pop-up list of additional items. Choose a filter from the pop-up menu. In most cases, once you select a filter, you can see a preview of the selected filter before you finalize your changes. Try the following example:

1. Choose the Artistic→Colored Pencil filter. A box appears with a preview window and boxes where you can enter numbers to set the Pencil Width, Stroke Pressure, and Paper Brightness. Type some numbers into the boxes or drag the sliders to change the settings. See the image on the left in Figure 2.6 for an example of the effect of the Colored Pencil filter.

2. Notice the effect of your choices in the preview window. Place your mouse inside the preview window. The pointer changes into a hand. Click, hold, and drag to move the picture around, previewing different parts of your image.

3. When you find the settings you like, click OK. Now you will see the effect this filter has on your entire image. If you decide you do not like the filter effect, go to the Edit menu and choose Undo. The effect will be removed.

There are many possibilities for adding and combining filter effects in your images. However, you should use them sparingly for maximum impact. Following are some ideas for how you might use some of the filters.

☆ Use a Blur filter to blur an image that will be placed in the background with text or other images on top of it. Adding Blur to the image will make it appear to recede into the background, making the foreground images easier to see. Adding Blur can also make the file size of your image smaller—the Web prefers blurred to sharp edges.

☆ A Distort filter can add some twists and twirls to your images. You might use the Glass filter on a photo of a window.

☆ The Noise→Add Noise filter can make an image that is too sharp, or digital in appearance, look more textured and artistic. Be careful, though, as too much Noise can make your image large in file size, which means it will take a long time to download. You can also try the Artistic→Film Grain filter for a similar effect.

☆ The Sketch→Chrome filter may be useful for adding a high-tech look to all or parts of your image. You should probably use the Image→Adjust→Levels command after applying this filter to add more white to your image.

☆ The Stylize→Wind filter may give your image the illusion of motion. This effect might be appropriate for sports-related photos.

Choose several filter effects and experiment to see what they do. You may want to make some notes to yourself about filter effects that you like but are unsure how to use at the moment.

(a)   (b)

Figure 2.6 (a) Image with the Artistic→Colored Pencil Filter Effect Applied (b) Image with a Colored Border of 20 Pixels

Using the Selection Tools

Don't go overboard with the use of filters. Consider your audience and your message before deciding to alter your images. Perhaps you should use a filter effect on only a certain portion rather than the entire image. To do so, you will use Photoshop's Selection tools.

Even when you are not using filters, sometimes you want to do something to only a part of your image rather than to the entire image. You can use the Selection tools in the Toolbox to select the part of your image that you want to modify. You can also use the Select menu in the Menu bar at the top of the screen to Select All, Deselect, Reselect, or select the Inverse of an area you have selected.

Using the Select Menu to Add a Border

Using the Select All menu command, it is easy to add a border that is as small as 1 pixel wide or as large as 200 pixels wide around the edges of your image. The following activity shows you how to use the Select menu to add a border to your image.

1. Choose a color for your border by clicking on the Background chip in the Toolbox and picking a color in the Color Picker. Go to the Select menu and choose All. You will see a selection box of marching ants around your image.

2. Go back to the Select menu and choose Modify→Border. In the Border Selection box that appears, type a Width of 20 pixels and click OK. You will see that the marching ants have receded into your image by 20 pixels on each side.

3. Click the [Delete] key on your keyboard. The part of your image around the edges is replaced with the color you selected, and it softly transitions from the border color into the image. For example, see the colored border applied to the image in Figure 2.6(b).

4. To remove the marching ants selection box, go back to the Select menu and choose Deselect.

Using the Selection Tools in the Toolbox

There are additional selection tools at the top of the left column in the Toolbox that allow you to select only a part of your image.

The default tool is the Rectangular Marquee tool. If you click and hold on that tool, a pop-up box shows you additional tools, including the Elliptical Marquee tool.

Choose either of those tools and then move your mouse to your image. Click, hold, and drag in a sweeping motion around part of the image. You are drawing a box or oval of marching ants around a selected part of the image.

The Lasso tool (the second tool down in the left column of the Toolbox) allows you to draw a freeform selection around an image. As you draw your selection, make sure that the end of your selection meets the beginning of your selection to Close the Path. The Lasso tool is useful when making irregularly shaped selections.

Using the Magic Wand (the second tool down on the right side of the Toolbox), you can click a part of an image to select all the similar pixels in that area. Use the Tolerance setting in the Options bar to increase or decrease the range of similar pixels that are selected. For example, you may wish to select all of the red parts of a flower and Fill them with another color.

Once you make a selection, you can do something to or with that selection. You can even Copy the selection (choose Copy in the Edit menu) and Paste it somewhere else.

☆ SHORTCUT **Constraining Proportions**

If you want to select a perfect square or a perfect circle with the Rectangular and the Elliptical Marquee tools, hold down the [Shift] key while you are dragging with the tool.

Clone Stamp Tool

An interesting method for copying part of an image and pasting it somewhere else is to use the Clone Stamp tool (sometimes referred to as the rubber stamp tool).

For this activity, use an image that has a recognizable element such as a face, a flower, a volleyball. Be sure that this element is not so large that it takes up the entire image space.

In the Toolbox, click the Clone Stamp tool (the fifth tool down from the top in the left-hand column). You will use this tool to select a part of your image and then paint with that part on another portion of the image.

1. With the Clone Stamp tool selected, move your mouse over the part of the image you wish to use as paint. Hold down the [Alt] key (Windows) or the [Option] key (Mac) while you click once with the Clone Stamp tool. Let go of the key and the mouse.

2. You have now identified the target area—the area you wish to use as paint.

3. Move your mouse to another portion of your image. Now click, hold, and drag. Try to constrain the movement of your mouse by holding your wrist down while moving the mouse with your fingers and thumb. (Good motor skills are important in using many of Photoshop's tools.)

4. You will see that you are painting, but instead of using a color, you are using a part of your image—the part you [Alt] or [Option] clicked on with the Clone Stamp tool.

5. While you were painting, you may have noticed that a cross hair appeared over the part you [Alt] or [Option] clicked on. Whatever the cross hair passes over is the part you are using as paint. Figure 2.7 shows the cross hair over the part used as paint, in this case the boy's head. A duplicate—or clone—of the boy's head was painted in the upper left of the photo.

Figure 2.7 Clone Stamp Tool in Action

The Clone Stamp tool can be very useful when you wish to add or subtract something from an image. For example, you may have a beautiful landscape image, but a big telephone pole is ruining it. You could clone some sky, grass, or trees to cover up the pole.

When you become more experienced, use Photoshop's Help menu for information on using advanced features of the Clone Stamp tool.

Advanced Editing Tools

Photoshop contains many other tools for editing your images. The Polygonal and Magnetic Lasso tools, the Healing Brush, and the Retouching tools, among others, are extremely useful for editing. You will find explanations of these tools in Chapter Eight. For now, try to master the tools and techniques presented in this chapter. Along with useful editing techniques, you will be learning the precise and sometimes difficult motor skills necessary to master the use of Photoshop's tools.

Using Photoshop Appropriately

Now that you've seen a little bit of what can be done with Photoshop, you will probably never again look at an image in print or on the Web the way you did before. From a positive perspective, using Photoshop is a great way to create compelling images even if you do not have a lot of skill or a background in design. From a negative perspective, you can see how easy it would be to create a false image and pass it off as the real thing.

This is a book about how to use Photoshop, not about the appropriateness of the content you can create using this program. However, here are a few words of caution.

☆ Generally, any time a person—including yourself—creates an original work and fixes it in a medium such as a document, an image file, a recording, and so on, the person automatically owns the copyright for that work, and the work may not be used or changed without the person's permission.

☆ You should not take all or part of someone else's work and use it in your own work without asking for their permission and/or paying a copyright licensing fee.

☆ You should not use someone else's name or likeness without obtaining their permission.

☆ See the end of this chapter for a URL for the Library of Congress Web site that discusses copyright issues.

◎◎ Saving a JPG Image for the Web

In Chapter One, you learned that the GIF format is best for images that are graphic in nature. The JPG format is best for photographs and images with subtle blends of color.

Now that you've learned to acquire and edit a photograph, you are ready to save it in the JPG format for the Web.

About Compression

When you save your image in the GIF or JPG format, you are compressing it. Generally, the following things happen during compression:

1. Certain pixels of the image that are the same—those in a blue background, for example—are stored only once and mathematically reproduced as needed when your image is actually displayed.

2. Parts of the image that are barely used—a few tiny pixels of a particular color that appear in only one or two places—are discarded and removed from the image forever.

Every time you save an image in the GIF or JPG format, it is compressed. For example, if you open a JPG image, edit it, save it, open it again, edit it, save it, open it again, edit it, and save it again, you will have compressed it three times. Each time, some of the image information is discarded. Eventually this recompression degrades the quality of your image.

This is another reason to use the saving strategy recommended earlier. If you always edit your images in the PSD (Photoshop) format and then save an Output copy in the JPG format using the Save for Web command, you will avoid the problems that repeated compression can cause.

Using the Save for Web Command

In Chapter One, you learned about many of the basic tools in the Save for Web box. You can refer to that discussion to refresh your memory if necessary. While you read the following section, refer to Figure 2.8, which shows the Save for Web box with JPG settings.

☆ **TIP**   **What's the Difference Between JPEG and JPG?**

JPEG stands for Joint Photographic Experts Group. Years ago, this group of people agreed on the type of image file that would be created using this computer format. JPEG has been shortened to JPG for use on the Web. You should not use JPEG to name your files for the Web—use JPG.

To save an Output image as JPG, follow these steps:

1. Go to the File menu and choose Save for Web. To save an image in the JPG format, choose JPEG in the top left pop-up box in the far right column of the Save for Web box. Refer to the settings shown in Figure 2.8.

2. Below the JPEG pop-up is another pop-up box with Low, Medium, High, and Maximum as the choices. These choices refer to quality. When you choose one of these settings, the number in the Quality box to the right will change.

Saving a JPG Image for the Web

Figure 2.8 Save for Web Box with JPG Settings

3. Experiment with different settings and notice the effect on your image. If you are in the 2-Up mode (choose the 2-Up tab at the top of the box), you will see your original on the left and the JPG image on the right.

4. Use the Zoom tool to magnify part of the JPG image. Compare the JPG to the original. Notice the download time at the bottom of the box. If the image will take too long to download, lower your quality settings.

5. Once you are satisfied with your choices, click OK, and save the image with a brief, lowercase name. Check to make sure that the JPG extension is automatically added to the file name.

☆ Summary

▷ When you scan an image, you should use the best-quality settings possible. Save a copy of your image to use when editing it for the Web.

▷ Photoshop contains many tools for adjusting your image after you have scanned it. You can crop, rotate, and sharpen your image. You can also adjust the contrast and color levels.

▷ The relationship between pixels, image size, and resolution is very important to the quality of your image.

▷ Photoshop includes many filters and tools you can use to enhance your images.

▷ You should save photographs and images with subtle blends of color in the JPG format for the Web.

☆ Online References

A few scanning tips
http://www.scantips.com

Photoshop Filters and Plug-ins
http://www.desktoppublishing.com/photoshopfilters.html

More than you ever wanted to know about the JPG format
http://www.jpeg.org/public/jpeghomepage.htm

HotWired's GIF versus JPG Q&A
http://hotwired.lycos.com/webmonkey/geektalk/97/30/index3a.html?tw=design

Browser Statistics from W3 Schools
http://www.w3schools.com/browsers/browsers_stats.asp

U.S. Copyright Office in the Library of Congress
http://www.copyright.gov/

What Is Resolution? From Wake Forest University
http://www.wfubmc.edu/biomed/infonotes/file_resolution.html

A source for stock photographs
http://www.corbis.com/

☆ Review Questions

1. Why should you scan and save an image at 150 dpi?
2. What is the proper dpi for an image that will be used on the Web?
3. What is the result of using Photoshop to enlarge the physical dimensions of a previously scanned image?
4. Why is it often better to crop an image than to simply reduce the overall size for use on the Web?

47

5. What is a pixel? What is its relationship to image size? To resolution?

6. What types of things might you do with the Clone Stamp tool?

7. What kinds of images should you save in the JPG format for the Web?

8. What happens when a file is compressed repeatedly?

☆ Hands-On Exercises

If you have access to the companion Web site for this book, use those files for the exercises.

1. Scan a photograph twice, once at 72 dpi and once at 150 dpi. Print each image from your desktop printer. Describe the differences in quality.

2. Purposely scan a photograph at a crooked angle. Use the Crop tool to straighten the image.

3. Using an image with a portion you would like to remove or cover up, use the Clone tool to paint something else in its place.

4. Take an image scanned at 72 dpi and one scanned at 150 dpi and save them each in the JPG format for the Web. Open a Web browser and use the File/Open command to open each of the images. Notice the differences in the way they are displayed. Explain.

5. Scan a photo and save it several times with different settings. In the Save for Web box, choose JPG and use several different Quality settings. Write down the effects each setting has on file size, download time, and overall quality.

CHAPTER THREE

CREATING GRAPHIC IMAGES

You've learned to acquire images from a variety of sources and edit them using Photoshop. In this chapter, you will learn to use Photoshop to create original graphic images that can be used for a logo, an icon, a button, or an image that will appear on your Web site.

◎◎ Chapter Objectives

☆ Learn some general information about graphic images

☆ Distinguish the difference between raster and vector graphics

☆ Learn more about color, and use background transparency

☆ Use basic tools in Photoshop to create logos, icons, and buttons

☆ Use Matte when saving a transparent GIF file

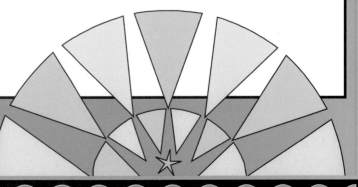

◎◎ General Information About Graphic Images

Here are a few tips to help you create interesting graphic images:

☆ Vector graphics give your images a sharp, professional, modern look.

☆ Choose your colors and color combinations wisely. Create a color guide for each of your projects.

☆ Learn to think small. Most logos, icons, and buttons used on the Web are less than 150 pixels wide and high.

☆ Use contrasts to gain effect—light/dark, big/small, thick/thin, soft/hard, and so on.

☆ Consider the content and purpose of your Web site and design with them in mind.

☆ Carry a sketchbook and some colored markers around with you. Draw interesting shapes and color combinations. Draw in your sketchbook every day.

☆ Observe the world around you. Begin to look at the space that surrounds objects as much as you look at the objects themselves. For example, consider the space within the handle of a coffee mug. Draw some interesting surrounding-space shapes.

☆ There are five basic shapes in everyday objects—dot, circle, straight line, curved line, and angle line. Use these shapes in your drawings.

Raster (Bitmap) Versus Vector Images

There are two main categories of images: **raster** (or bitmap) and **vector**.

Raster (bitmap) images are made up of pixels. Each pixel has a color and a specific location in the image. When you edit the image, you are editing the pixels in the image. When you enlarge a raster image, the pixels can become jagged and make your image look fuzzy.

Programs like Photoshop that work with raster images are sometimes called *painting programs*.

Vector images are considered **objects**. That is, they are made up of lines and curves that can be defined mathematically. Because they are based on mathematical formulas, vector images can be enlarged or scaled to any size and still look crisp and sharp. See Figure 3.1 and compare it with the enlarged raster image in Figure 3.2.

Programs that work with vector images are sometimes called *drawing programs*.

Photoshop includes both painting and drawing tools, though it is primarily a painting program. You can use full-featured drawing programs like Adobe Illustrator and Macromedia Freehand for advanced work with vector images. Macromedia Flash also contains an array of vector graphic tools.

Figure 3.1 Closeup of a Vector Image That Has Been Enlarged with the Image Size Box

Figure 3.2 Closeup of a Raster Image That Has Been Enlarged with the Image Size Box

For a novice Web designer, Photoshop gives you the primary tools you need to create and edit either category of images. In this chapter, we use a combination of painting and drawing tools to create graphics for original logos, icons, and buttons.

First, more about color and file types.

More Essentials About Color, GIF, and JPG Images

In Chapter One, you used painting tools to create a color guide and saved it in both the PSD (Photoshop) and GIF formats. The PSD image is your Project image—you can go back later and edit this image using all the special features of Photoshop. The GIF image is your Output file to be used on your Web site. Normally, you should not edit a GIF image.

Also in Chapter One, you learned about Photoshop's color modes. You used the RGB mode to create your color guide. When you saved your image as a GIF file, the saving process changed the color mode to indexed color—a palette of only 256 or fewer colors.

By limiting the total colors in a GIF image, you are reducing the file size, making the image download faster on a Web page.

When you used the Save for Web command to create the GIF file, you may have noticed the Color Table in the Save box. The Color Table consists of 16 rows and 16 columns, resulting in 256 squares. Each square contains a specific color. GIF images contain no more than 256 colors.

Learning More About Indexed Color

To become familiar with the Color Table in a GIF image, follow these procedures:

1. Choose File➔Open and select your colorguide.gif file.

2. Once the image is open, go to Image➔Mode and notice that there is a check-mark beside the term Indexed Color.

3. Farther down the Image➔Mode menu, choose Color Table. A box will open, showing you a table of up to 256 colors that make up all the colors in your GIF image.

4. Advanced users can create custom **index palettes**, adding and deleting certain colors and applying a particular palette to a series of images to achieve a uniform effect. As you become more experienced, you can use Photoshop's Help menu to learn how to generate a custom color table.

In Chapter One, you learned that GIF images are appropriate for graphics with blocks of solid color and shapes or text with hard edges. JPG images are appropriate for photographs with gradations of thousands or millions of multiple colors.

Viewing the Effect of Saving a Photograph as a GIF Image

Now you will perform an experiment to see the effect of reducing the number of colors in a photograph.

1. Choose File➔Open and select a *photograph* (not a graphic) that you acquired and saved as a PSD file in chapter two.

2. Choose File➔Save for Web. When the Save box opens, click the 2-Up tab at the top left of the box. You will see the PSD file on the left and the Output file you are creating on the right.

3. On the far-right side of the Save box, choose GIF from the pop-up menu in the left column. The Color Table will appear, showing you the palette of 256 colors available for the final image.

4. On the far-left side of the Save box, choose the Zoom tool and click on a portion of your image to magnify it. Use the hand tool to move around the photograph. Find areas of the photo where there are obvious differences between the original PSD file and the GIF file. Figure 3.3 shows the difference between the original image and the image that would result if a GIF palette were used.

5. You can also experiment with the pop-up box that shows different types of palettes (Perceptual, Selective, Adaptive, Web) and the Colors box where you can reduce the number of colors available for the image. When you make these choices, notice the changes to the Color Table and to the image.

6. Advanced users may also use types of Diffusion and Dither to alter the colors in their image. As a novice, you should probably concentrate on making your image look as good as possible to the human eye. Later, you can learn more of the details in advanced methods and terminology.

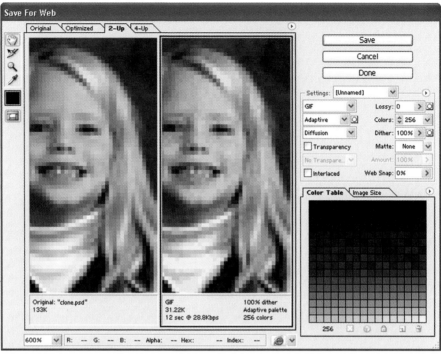

Figure 3.3 2-Up Setting in the Save for Web Box Showing the Original Photo and the Photo with a GIF Palette

You can see that reducing the number of colors available to a photograph may greatly lessen the quality of the image. In most cases, a photograph should not be saved as a GIF image.

☆ **TIP**   **Magnifying a Portion of an Image**

It is often useful to magnify the display of a portion of an image while you are working on it. Choose the Zoom tool from the Toolbox (bottom right above the color chips) and click on the portion of the image you wish to magnify.

The Save for Web box contains its own Zoom tool for use in examining an image before you save it.

When you use one of the Zoom tools, you are magnifying only the display of the image on the screen so that you can work closely on it. You are not altering the actual physical size of the image.

◎◎ Using Transparency

You've learned that GIF images are appropriate for graphics; they are usually smaller in file size than JPG images; and they contain a particular color palette of up to 256 colors.

Another feature of the GIF image format is that GIF images may contain areas that do not include any color at all. Those areas are **transparent** and "show through" to any color or image the GIF file is placed on. JPG images do not allow for this feature.

Transparency is a useful feature for Web designers.

Setting Up Your Work Area for Using Transparency

Before you begin to work with transparent images, you should set up the work area so that you will be able to see the transparent areas of your images.

1. Go to the Preferences menu and choose Transparency & Gamut.

2. In the Transparency Settings area, be sure that the choice for Grid Size is other than None. Usually, Medium works best.

3. For Grid Colors, choose Light.

These settings will allow you to see the areas of your image that will be transparent.

Creating a New Transparent Image

Begin this activity by creating a new image with a transparent background.

1. Create a new image by choosing File→New. Make the Width 50 pixels and the Height 50 pixels.

2. Be sure the resolution is 72 pixels per inch.

3. Set the mode to RGB color.

4. In the Contents area at the bottom of the New box, choose Transparent.

5. Click OK, and your new image will appear in the Photoshop work area.

☆ **TIP**   **About the RGB Color Mode**

Even though your Output file will be a GIF in the Indexed Color mode, you should create your original PSD file in the RGB Color mode. More of Photoshop's special editing features will be available to you in the RGB mode of a PSD file.

Drawing a Vector Image

In Chapter One, you used Photoshop's Brush tool to add colors to your image. You were *painting* and creating a raster or bitmap image. Now you will create a vector image while you learn about transparency.

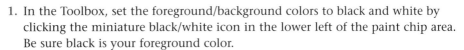

1. In the Toolbox, set the foreground/background colors to black and white by clicking the miniature black/white icon in the lower left of the paint chip area. Be sure black is your foreground color.

2. In the Toolbox, choose the Rectangle shape tool in the lower right column. Usually, the Rectangle tool is the default choice, but if you click and hold the tool, a fly-out menu appears, showing you additional choices (Rounded Rectangle, Ellipse, Polygon, Line, and Custom Shape).

3. Be sure the Shape Layers button is selected at the top left of the Options bar. If you are unsure which button is the Shape Layers button, hold your mouse over the button until a box appears with the name of the button.

4. Click, hold, and drag on your image to draw a rectangle. Draw within most but not all of the image area with your rectangle. When you let go of the mouse, the rectangle will appear and will be filled with the foreground color.

5. Assuming that you did not take up the entire image area with your rectangle, you can see the transparent area (denoted by the gray and white grid boxes) around your image.

Now use your imagination a bit. Maybe you have a Web page that has the color red as a background color. The black rectangle you've just created will be a navigation button. If the area around your rectangle is transparent and you save your image as a transparent GIF file, then the black rectangle will sit on top of the red background of your Web page with no other surrounding color.

If you were to save this image as a JPG file (in which transparency is not supported), a white background would automatically be inserted around your black rectangle. See Figure 3.4 for examples of how your button would look with no transparency (left) and with transparency (right).

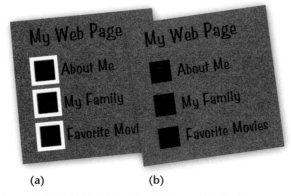

(a)   (b)

Figure 3.4 (a) Web Navigation Buttons with No Transparency
(b) Same Buttons with Transparent Background

At the end of this chapter, you will learn exactly how to save a GIF image with Transparency using the Save for Web command.

Using Transparency

Basic Tools for Creating Web Graphics

Photoshop contains many tools for creating graphics. In this section, you will learn more about the Shape tools, as well as the Pen tool. Both tools allow you to create vector graphics.

The Styles palette and the Transform tools allow you to add interesting effects to your graphics.

The Painting tools allow you to work with many types of brushes and a Pencil tool to create raster graphics. Photoshop also contains an Eraser tool that allows you to erase parts of a raster image.

Using the Shape Tools for Vector Graphics

Usually, logos, icons, and buttons used on a Web site range from 35 to 150 pixels in width and height.

Go to the File→New menu and create a new image that you can use for experimenting with the Shape tools. Make your image at least 200 pixels wide by 200 pixels high so that you will have room to experiment. Set your resolution to 72 and choose Transparent Background.

You've already used the Rectangle Shape tool, so choose another Shape tool for this image. Figure 3.5 shows the toolbox with the Shape Tool submenu.

First, choose a foreground color. You may also want to open your Info palette, also shown in Figure 3.5, by choosing the Window→Info menu item. The Info palette will show you the size, in pixels, of your shape as you are drawing it. Figure 3.5 shows a circle drawn with the Ellipse Shape tool.

☆**TIP**   **Loading Additional Shapes into the Custom Shapes Box**

If there are not very many shapes available in your Custom Shapes box, click the right-pointing triangle menu at the top right of the Shapes box. Choose **All** from the pop-up menu that appears. Additional shapes will be loaded into your Shapes box.

Now create a custom shape.

1. Choose the Custom Shape tool in the Toolbox. Notice that the Options bar at the top of your work area includes a box labeled Shape with a corresponding icon and a downward-pointing triangle. Click the triangle to reveal a set of custom shapes available to you. Select a shape by clicking it.

2. Be sure the Shape Layers button is selected at the top left of the Options bar. If you are unsure which button is the Shape Layers button, hold your mouse over the button until a box appears with the name of the button.

3. Click, hold, and drag on your image to begin drawing the shape.

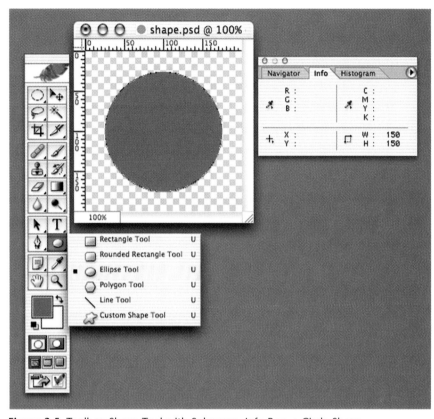

Figure 3.5 Toolbox Shape Tool with Submenu, Info Box, a Circle Shape

4. Notice the Width and Height expressed in pixels in the Info palette.
5. When you have drawn the shape to the size you want, let go of the mouse.
6. The shape, in the color you specified in the Foreground Color chip, appears on your image.

☆ **WARNING** **Jagged Edges**

When you first complete your shape drawing, it may look as if it has jagged edges. In its final form, however, it will be a smooth-edged graphic.

☆ **TIP** **Constraining Proportions**

Hold down the [Shift] key while you are drawing a shape to constrain its proportions. For example, if you want a perfect circle, hold the [Shift] key while you draw with the Ellipse tool.

Each of the Shape tools has additional options that can be chosen by clicking the downward-pointing triangle next to the shapes icons in the Options bar. As you become more experienced, you can use Photoshop's Help menu to learn more about the tool options.

Save your image as a PSD file and create more new images. Experiment with each of the main Shape tools and a few of the Custom Shape tools, using different colors and proportions.

Using the Pen Tools

The Pen tools allow you to create sophisticated vector images. At first, it is difficult to master the use of the Pen tools, but if you stay with it, you will learn to create amazing shapes.

Drawing Linear Shapes with the Pen Tool

1. Select the Pen tool from the lower left side of the Toolbox.

2. Click on your image to set your first **anchor point**.

3. Release the mouse and click on another area of your image to set a second anchor point. Photoshop draws a line, or **path**, between your two anchor points.

4. Again click on another part of the image to set a third anchor point perpendicular to the path you already created. The area between the points is filled with your foreground color.

5. Return the mouse to your first anchor point and notice that your mouse pointer shows the Pen tool with a circle beside it. Click the first anchor point to completely close the path you have created with your three anchor points.

6. Your shape will look as if it has jagged edges now, but it will look crisp and smooth when you save the image.

☆ SHORTCUT **Selecting the Pen Tool**

To quickly select the Pen tool, press the P key on your keyboard.

You've just created a simple, linear shape with the Pen tool. Now create another new image to learn how to use the Pen tool to create curved shapes.

Drawing Curves with the Pen Tool

1. Create a New image and select the Pen tool from the Toolbox.

2. Click once somewhere on the image and release the mouse.

3. On another part of your image, click, hold, and drag with the Pen tool. Don't let go of the mouse yet. As you drag, two handles will appear. Keep dragging and you will see that you are creating a curved shape between your first anchor point and your second anchor point. Figure 3.6(a) shows the Pen Tool in action. At the top left is the first anchor point. Notice the curve created between the first and second anchor points.

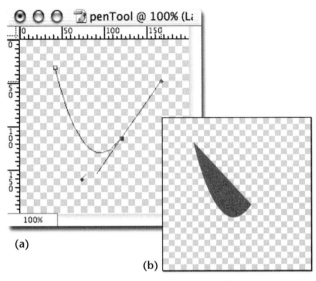

(a)

(b)

Figure 3.6 (a) Pen Tool in Action (b) Resulting Shape

4. Click and drag a few more places on the image. You will notice that the farther you drag your anchor point, the more extreme is your curve.

5. When you are finished making curves, click the first anchor point to close the path you have created. Figure 3.6(b) shows the resulting shape created by the action shown on the left.

Drawing with the Freeform Pen Tool

1. Create a new image. In the Toolbox, click and hold the Pen tool and choose Freeform Pen tool from the fly-out menu.

2. Click, hold, and drag on your image to draw a freeform shape of your choosing. Release the mouse.

Refining Your Pen Tool Paths

You can use some additional settings and methods to adjust the paths you create with the Pen tools.

☆ With the basic Pen tool selected, notice the downward-pointing triangle next to the Shapes box in the Options bar. Click the triangle and click to check Rubber Band. Click several times on your image to create paths. Notice that your mouse has a line attached to it. The line moves like a rubber band that is being stretched and contracted. This line gives you a preview of the next path you will create when you click the mouse again. To complete an image and disconnect the Rubber Band, hold down the [Control] key (Windows) or Command ⌘ key (Mac) and click on the image.

☆ With the Freeform Pen tool selected, click the triangle next to the Shapes box in the Options bar and adjust the Curve Fit by entering a pixel amount between 0.5 and 10.0. Draw a shape. Make a different adjustment to the Curve Fit and draw another shape. Entering higher amounts in the Curve Fit box means you will create simpler paths with fewer anchor points.

☆ To change the color of a shape you have created, double-click inside the image of the shape in the Layers palette (go to the Window→Layers menu if you need to open the Layers palette). When the Color Picker appears, choose a new color to Fill your shape.

☆ To modify your shape, be sure you have *closed the path* by Ctrl-clicking (Windows) or ⌘-clicking (Mac) on the image. Immediately above the Pen tool in the Toolbox is an Arrow tool. Click and hold and select the Direct Selection tool from the fly-out menu. Click on an edge of the shape to reveal the anchor points. Choose an anchor point, click, hold, and drag to change the shape. In Figure 3.7(a), the blue area denotes the shape originally drawn. You can see how an anchor point has been moved upward to change the shape. Figure 3.7(b) shows the resulting shape.

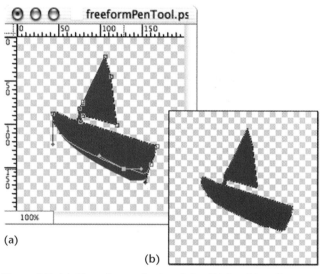

(a)

(b)

Figure 3.7 (a) Changing an Anchor Point (b) Resulting Shape

☆**WARNING** Pen Tools

Using the Pen tools can be frustratingly difficult for a beginner. If you find that you are unable to create acceptable shapes with the Pen tools, use the prebuilt and custom shape tools for your graphic images.

Using the Styles Palette

Photoshop contains many prebuilt **styles** that you can apply to your shapes to make them appear more interesting. You can apply styles to many types of images. In Chapter Four, you will learn how to modify the prebuilt styles and create and save your own styles.

Most of the prebuilt styles are especially useful for Web buttons. The styles add depth and dimension to shapes used as clickable buttons.

1. Choose File➔New to create a new image. Choose a prebuilt shape like the Rectangle and draw it onto your image.

2. If it is not already open, choose the Window➔Styles menu to open the Styles palette.

3. Figure 3.8 shows the Styles palette. In it, you see several small shapes, each with different colors and attributes, or styles. Choose one of the shapes by clicking it.

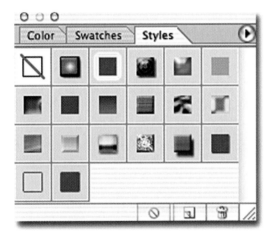

Figure 3.8 Styles Palette

4. Notice that the shape you drew has taken on the style of the shape in the Styles palette.

5. To remove a style, click the Default Style shape—a white box with a diagonal red line through it.

6. Experiment by adding other styles to your shape. Styles can add a professional look to your Web graphics.

Transforming Shapes

Photoshop provides several tools for transforming your image. You can make the image larger or smaller, rotate it, skew or distort it. You can flip it horizontally or vertically. You can use precise measurements to achieve these effects, or you can make the transformations by freely dragging to get the look you want.

☆ **TIP**   **About the Canvas**

In Chapter Two, you learned to use the Image→Rotate Canvas tools to change the orientation of your entire image. Think of the canvas as if you were an artist. The canvas is a work area with a fixed size and orientation. The artist paints on the canvas—and sometimes paints on top of a previously painted area. The paint is separate from the canvas and can be applied in any direction.

The same is true in Photoshop. The canvas is the entire work area for the image. When you paint on or add a shape to your image work area, it is similar to adding paint on an artist's canvas. The paint or shape is separate from the canvas and can be changed, moved, or oriented in any direction.

Here are some tips for using the Distort tool.

1. Create a new image, add a shape to it, and apply a style if you wish. Be sure to allow plenty of canvas room around the shape. This will give you room to experiment with transforming your shape.

2. Choose Edit→Transform and notice the fly-out menu. There are several options for transforming, or changing, the shape you created. Choose Distort and release the mouse.

3. You will see that a box appears around your image. There are small squares at each corner of the box and in the middle of each side of the box.

4. When you place your mouse over one of the boxes in Distort, you will notice that an arrowhead appears.

5. Place your mouse over one of the boxes, click, hold, and drag. You are distorting the shape. Figure 3.9 shows the Distort tool in action.

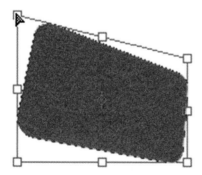

Figure 3.9 Distort Tool in Action

6. When you are ready to finalize the transformation, double-click inside the boxed area. You can also click the Commit button, denoted by a large check-mark at the far right of the Options bar. If you do not wish to commit to a transformation, click the Cancel icon to the left of the Commit button.

7. Experiment with the other transformation tools. There will be slight differences in the appearance of the corner and middle boxes, and you will use them differently.

Using the Painting Tools for Raster Graphics

When you worked with the Shape tools, you were creating vector graphics. The Painting tools create raster (bitmap) graphics.

In Chapter One, you worked with the Brush tool, which creates raster graphics. You selected different sizes and shapes of brushes in the Options menu. Now you will learn to use some of Photoshop's other Painting tools.

To experiment with the Painting tools, create a new image and select a foreground color.

Using the Pencil Tool

First try using the Pencil tool.

1. Click and hold the Brush tool icon and select the Pencil tool from the fly-out menu.

2. Set the Brush size to 1.

3. Click and drag on your image.

4. Use the Zoom tool to magnify your image as much as possible.

⭐ **SHORTCUT Selecting the Zoom Tool**

To quickly select the Zoom tool, press the Z key on your keyboard.

Notice that the Pencil tool creates very distinct squares, or pixels, of color on your image. The Pencil tool comes in handy when you are creating very small icons or editing a very small portion of an image.

Using the Airbrush Tool

Now try the Airbrush tool.

1. Create a new image and select the Brush tool in the Toolbox.

2. Notice that on the Options bar there is an icon that allows you to use your Brush tool as an airbrush.

3. Click the Airbrush icon on the Options bar, and paint on your image.

4. You can adjust the Flow of the airbrush in the box next to the Airbrush icon to make the spray heavier or lighter.

Notice the differences in painting with the normal Brush tool, the Airbrush, and the Pencil tool.

There are many advanced methods for using the Brush and Airbrush tools. As you experiment, you can use Photoshop's Help menu to learn more about specialized options.

☆**WARNING** **Location of the Airbrush Tool**

In older versions of Photoshop, the Airbrush tool appears in the Toolbox. In newer versions of Photoshop, when you select the Brush tool from the Toolbox, an Airbrush button appears in the Options bar.

Using the Eraser Tools

If you make a mistake with any of the Painting tools, you can correct it.

1. On the image that is open, decide on an area of color you would like to erase. (If you do not have an open image, create a new image and use one of the Painting tools to create an area of color.)

2. Select the Eraser tool in the Toolbox.

3. On the Options bar, select a mode—Brush, Pencil, or Block—from the pop-up menu. You can even select the Airbrush tool to use as an eraser. Experiment with all the Eraser modes.

4. Click, hold, and drag on part of the image to erase it.

There are many advanced methods for using the Eraser tools. As you experiment, you can use Photoshop's Help menu to learn more about specialized erasing options.

The Painting and Shape tools allow you to create graphics with specific shapes in interesting colors and styles. Spend some time experimenting with these tools and think about how you might use them to create logos, icons, buttons, and other graphics for your Web site.

◉◉ Saving a Graphic with a Transparent Background for the Web

If you have been working with images that have a transparent background, you are ready to save one of your graphics for the Web.

If none of the images you created in this chapter have a transparent background, stop and make one now. Choose File→New. Set the size at 200 pixels wide and high, the resolution at 72, the mode as RGB, and the Contents as Transparent. Use the Shape or Painting tools to create a shape. Be sure there is some transparent background space around the shape. Save it in the PSD format.

Using Matte When Saving a Transparent GIF File

You may want to review the end of Chapter One, which includes general information about using the Save for Web command to save a GIF image. The following activity introduces some additional features of the Save for Web box.

1. With your image open in Photoshop, choose File➔Save for Web.

2. As you did in Chapter One, choose the 2-Up setting from the tab at the top of the box. Choose GIF from the pop-up menu in the far-right side of the box.

3. Your PSD file will appear on the left with its transparent background noted by the gray and white checkerboard pattern. The GIF file you are saving appears on the right.

4. In the left column of the far right side, you will see a box for checking Transparency On or Off. If it is On, check it Off now.

5. Notice that your GIF file now has a white background. If you do not check Transparency On, and if None is selected as the Matte color, a white background will automatically be inserted behind your image.

6. Check Transparency On now. Next to the box called Matte on the right side, click the downward-pointing triangle. You will see several color choices.

7. If you know the background color of the Web page where your GIF image will be placed, choose that color as your Matte color. By doing so, your image will blend seamlessly into the background color. There will be no distracting **halo**—or white edge—around the image.

8. Often, choosing a Matte color helps eliminate a jagged appearance on the edges of a transparent GIF. Even if you created your image as a vector graphic in Photoshop, the process of making the image into a GIF file will *rasterize* the image. Raster graphics are more subject to problems with the jaggies than vector graphics.

9. Experiment with different combinations of Transparency On/Off and Matte None/Color. Use the Zoom tool to magnify your image and watch the changes to the edges as you select different Transparency and Matte options.

Figure 3.10 shows a comparison of Transparency and Matte settings.

You've learned to acquire, create, and edit images in Photoshop. You know how to save images for the Web as JPG, GIF, and transparent GIF files. In the next chapter you will learn to use Photoshop's Text tools along with some more advanced methods for creating interesting images.

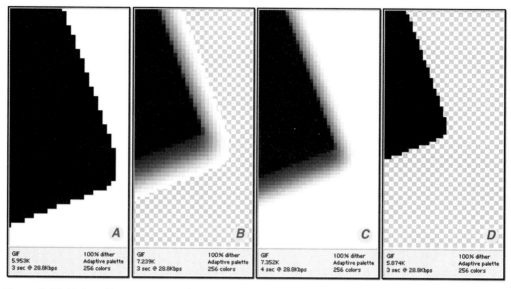

Figure 3.10 Various Transparency and Matte Settings in the Save for Web Box; (a) Transparency Off/Matte: None; (b) Transparency On/Matte: White; (c) Transparency Off/Matte: White; (d) Transparency On/Matte: None

☆ Summary

▷ Raster images are based on pixels and are created with Painting tools. Vector images are based on mathematical formulas and are created with Drawing or Shape tools.

▷ The GIF file format contains a maximum of only 256 colors. The GIF format should not normally be used for saving photographs.

▷ The GIF file format supports Transparency.

▷ There are many tools for creating graphics, including the Shape tools, Pen tools, and Brushes. You can also transform your images by scaling, rotating, skewing, and distorting. You can add a prebuilt style to a shape to give it certain types of shading and depth.

▷ When you save a transparent GIF image, you can add a Matte color to prevent jagged edges or a halo on the image.

☆ Online References

HOW Magazine
`http://www.howdesign.com/`

Photoshop Tutorial
`http://www.adobe.com/web/tips/phsrbvectorshapes/main.html`

Bloomsburg University Virtual Training Center
`http://iit.bloomu.edu/vthc/Photoshop/DRAWING/vectorshapes.htm`

Fun with vector shapes in Photoshop from Adobe
`http://www.adobe.com/web/tips/phsrbvectorshapes/main.html`

Symbols.com
`http://www.symbols.com`

The Design and Publishing Center on Vector Graphics
`http://www.graphic-design.com/Photoshop/tutorials/0402-23.html`

Raster vs. Vector Images from Wake Forest School of Medicine
`http://www.wfubmc.edu/biomed/infonotes/raster_vector.html`

☆ Review Questions

1. Explain the primary difference between a raster image and a vector image.

2. Which type of image—GIF or JPG—supports Transparency?

3. Which tools—Painting tools or Shape tools—do you use to create a vector graphic? Explain the difference between these two types of tools.

4. What does the Matte setting in the Save for Web box do? When might you use a Matte color?

5. How many colors are possible in a GIF image?

6. What is the downside to saving a photograph in the GIF format? Explain why this is so.

7. How can you use contrast to make eye-catching graphics?

8. Name three Transform tools and explain why you would use them.

☆ Hands-On Exercises

If you have access to the companion Web site for this book, use those files for the exercises.

1. Scan a photo at 72 dpi. Using Photoshop's Image Size box, enlarge the image by four or five times the amount in the Image Size box and save a copy of the enlarged image. Open both images and compare quality. Use the Zoom tool to magnify portions of the photos and notice the differences between the two photos. Now create a vector image using one of the Shape tools. Enlarge the vector image by four or five times, magnify the image, and compare it with the original. Compare the differences between the enlarged photo and the enlarged vector image.

2. Create a new image with a transparent background. Create a shape for a Web page button. Add a style to the shape. Save the image as a transparent GIF file. Create three or four more buttons with different styles. Save the buttons with different Transparency and Matte settings, and compare the results.

3. Compare the result of using the Brush tool with a setting of 1 to the result of using the Pencil tool set at size 1. Use the Zoom tool to magnify the images as much as possible to see the results. Try other Brush shapes and sizes and magnify the display of the images to compare the results.

4. Open a photograph you have saved as a PSD file. Save for Web as a JPG file and then again as a GIF file. Save several copies of each with different settings. Compare the results.

5. Create a new image and add a shape. Use one of the Transform tools to alter the shape. Save a copy of the image and try another of the Transform tools. Repeat, using as many transforming tools as possible.

CHAPTER FOUR

USING TEXT, LAYERS, EFFECTS, AND STYLES

Y ou've learned to acquire and edit photographs and create original graphic shapes. With the addition of text, layers, and effects, your images will take on more dimension and communicate more information. *Text* can be used to create an eye-catching headline or to put words on top of shapes that will become Web page buttons. *Layers*, one of the most powerful and useful features in Photoshop, are used to separate elements of your image. This not only makes editing easier but lets you create complex and compelling images. *Effects and styles* can be added to text and layers to make them stand out and appear to pop off the page.

Chapter Objectives

⭐ Learn basic information about text on the Web

⭐ Use Photoshop's Text tools

⭐ Use Layers—one of Photoshop's most powerful tools

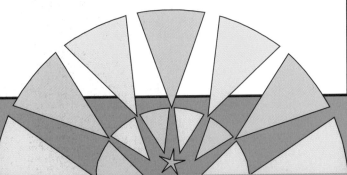

☆ Use Effects and Styles to make your images more interesting

☆ Gain a deeper understanding of the PSD file format

◎◎ Text on the Web: Basic Principles

Generally, the text you see on a Web page is one of two types: **live text** or **image text**. You use Photoshop to create image text. As a Web designer, you will have to decide which type of text is most appropriate for each element of your Web page. When you know you will need image text, you will use Photoshop to create it. When you have bodies of text that you know will be live text, you can use Photoshop to make a *mock-up* of it to help you as you design your Web page.

Live Text

Live text is typed into Web page editing software or typed directly within the code of an HTML document. When a user views a Web page, the fonts used to display live text on a Web page come from the user's computer. The fonts are not embedded into the Web page. The Web page merely contains instructions for the browser to use fonts from the user's computer to display the live text.

Following are some characteristics of live text:

☆ When a computer does not have the particular font designated in the code of a Web page, it will use a substitute font to display the page.

☆ Certain properties of the text may be altered by settings in the user's computer and Web browser.

☆ Some of the characteristics of HTML code may limit the ways in which you display text on a Web page.

☆ Live text can be used for any part of a Web page. It is especially useful for large bodies of text on a page.

☆ Live text downloads quickly and thus is very useful for creating Web pages.

☆ Live text can be searched and thus identified by search engines; it can be hyperlinked; it can be styled with a popular HTML method for formatting text called cascading style sheets; it can be copied and pasted by the viewer.

☆ Live text appears differently on different computers. When using live text, designers must relinquish some control over their design.

Image Text

Image text is prepared in a program like Photoshop and saved as an image file. Image text can appear alone or with a graphic or a photograph. Text that is part of an image file is fixed in place; it is not dependent on the user's computer or fonts for display on a Web page.

Following are some characteristics of image text:

⭐ Web designers use image text when they want to control the display of text on a Web page.

⭐ Using image text allows you to use special fonts that users may not have on their computers.

⭐ Using image text allows you to design attractive text layouts that would be impossible to create within the constraints of an HTML document.

⭐ Web designers often use image text for navigation buttons, headlines, logos, a company's name, and other small bits of text.

⭐ Image text downloads more slowly than live text. Thus, it should be used sparingly on a Web page.

Text on the Screen Versus Text on the Printed Page

Users read and respond to text displayed on a computer screen differently than to text on the printed page. The type of text that is used on a Web page is an important consideration in your design. Most Web designers choose carefully between serif fonts and sans serif fonts when they are creating a Web page.

In Figure 4.1, you can see that the **serif font** has small curves—serifs—at the ends of each letter that help carry the eye from one letter to the next. On the printed page, the serifs help us read more fluidly.

However, when viewing a Web page on a computer screen, the serifs in a large body of text can blur and make the text difficult to read. Generally, you should not use serif fonts for large bodies of text on a Web page.

In Figure 4.1 you can see that the **sans serif font** does not have extra curves on the letters. On both the printed page and on the screen, these fonts stand out and are easy to scan and read quickly.

Figure 4.1 Serif and Sans Serif Fonts

Generally, you should use sans serif fonts for buttons, small images, and large bodies of text on a Web page.

Following are some guidelines for using text on the Web:

⭐ Text in small sizes can be more difficult to read on a screen than similarly sized text on a printed page.

☆ Large bodies of text on a screen can tire a user's eyes.

☆ Most users do not want to read huge amounts of text on a screen.

☆ Web pages capture and keep a user's attention when the content includes short paragraphs and/or bulleted lists rather than large, dense paragraphs. Many Web designers use sans serif fonts for paragraph and list text. Often, this type of text is live text.

☆ Large, fluid, serif fonts are often used for headlines, a company's name, and other short, important bits of text. This text may be prepared as image text and combined with colors and shapes to create a particular design.

☆ Sans serif fonts are often used for navigation buttons. Navigation buttons are often created as image text so that the designer can control the display of the text and use special effects to make the buttons stand out.

☆ To improve the readability of any text on the Web, make sure you have a good contrast between the color of the text and the color or pattern of the background.

☆ **WARNING   Using Serif Fonts with Large Bodies of Text**

Sometimes, when a Web page contains an unusually large amount of dense text, designers may use a medium- or large-size serif font with lots of white space around the text. This design may help ensure readability on the screen, and it will be effective if the user prints out the page. (See the URL for MSNBC.com at the end of this chapter.)

Be careful with this design, however. If you are not exactly sure what you are doing, use a sans serif font for large bodies of text on your Web page.

◉◎ Text Tool in Photoshop

Using text creatively is one of the great joys of being a Web designer. Words, sentences, and paragraphs of text communicate in the most straightforward way possible. Attractive, eye-catching text captures the attention of viewers and leads them through the information you present on your Web page.

Photoshop's Text tool allows you to create an infinite variety of eye-catching text.

Using the Text Tool

To experiment with the Text tool, create a new image. Make the Contents of your new image white.

The Photoshop Toolbox contains a Text tool, denoted by the letter T, for creating text. When you click the Text tool, the Options bar reveals tools you can use to style your text.

To quickly select the Text tool, press the T key on your keyboard.

Figure 4.2 shows the Text tool and its fly-out menu, as well as the Options bar with the Text tool options. Choose the Text tool and look at the Options bar. You will see boxes where you can choose the font, the size, and other properties of the text. Toward the right end of the Options bar is a box of color. You can use this box as a color picker to choose a color for your text. By default, this box contains the same color as the Foreground Color chip in the Toolbox, but if you click the box in the Options bar, you can choose another color.

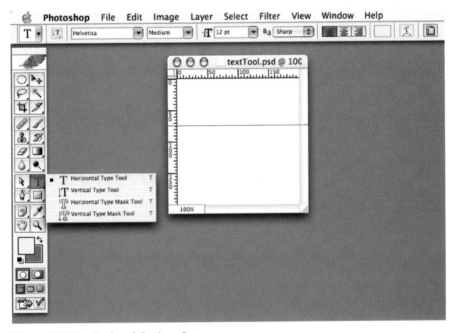

Figure 4.2 Text Tool and Options Bar

Whenever you use the Text tool, a new layer is automatically created. You will learn more about layers later in this chapter. See Figure 4.3, which shows the Layers palette with a new Text Layer.

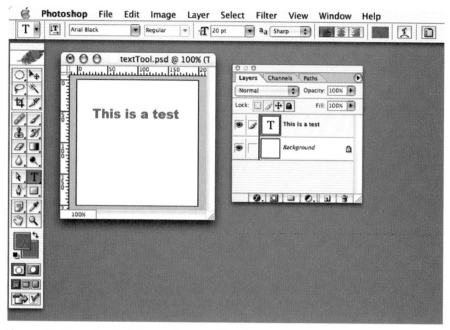

Figure 4.3 Using the Text Tool to Create a New Layer in the Layers Palette

Creating Text

1. Choose the Text tool in the Toolbox.
2. Use the Options bar to choose a font, a font size, and a font color. Click anywhere on your image. Type a word or a short line of text.
3. If your Layers palette is not open, go to Windows→Layers to open it now. Notice that when you typed text onto your image, it appeared in a separate layer above your original layer.
4. Finalize your text by clicking the Commit button—a checkmark at the far right of the Options bar—or by choosing another tool in the Toolbox.

Changing Properties for Text

1. With the Text tool still selected, click, hold, and drag across your text to select all of it.
2. Use the boxes in the Options bar to change one of the properties.
3. Select only one letter of your text. Change one of the properties. If your text contains more than one word, select one of the words and change the properties. As you can see, you can set different properties for each letter in a word or for each word in a sentence.
4. Commit your changes.

Orienting Text Horizontally or Vertically

1. With the Text tool still selected, select all your text.
2. On the Options bar, click the Text Orientation button to the left of the font box.
3. Your text will now be oriented vertically. You can still change any of the other properties of your text.
4. Commit your changes. See the example at left in Figure 4.4.

Figure 4.4 Left: Vertically Oriented Text; Center: Text Warped in the Flag Style; Right: Text Along a Path (Photoshop CS or Later Versions Only)

Warping Text into Different Shapes

1. Change your text back to a horizontal orientation.
2. While your text is selected, click the Warp Text tool to the right of the color box on the Options bar.
3. In the Warp Text box, choose a style from the pop-up menu. Use the default settings or enter your own distortion percentages. Click OK.
4. Commit your changes. See the example in the center of Figure 4.4.

Creating Text Along a Path (Photoshop CS or Later Version)

1. Use the Pen tool or a Shape tool to create a path or a shape.
2. Select the Text tool and click the bottom, or baseline, of the text cursor on the edge of the path or shape.
3. Type a word or a sentence.
4. Your text will follow the path or the shape.
5. Commit your changes. See the example at right in Figure 4.4.

Single-Line Text and Paragraph Text

You can use the Text tool to create a **single line** of text or **paragraph text**. When you use single-line text, you will have to use the Return (Enter) key on the keyboard to go down to the next line. When you use paragraph text, the text automatically flows from line to line, and you can resize the body of text to adjust the line flow.

Creating Single-Line Text

1. Select the Text tool.

2. Click once on your image.

3. Type a word, phrase, or body of text.

Creating Paragraph Text

1. Select the Text tool.

2. Click, hold, and drag on your image. You are drawing a "bounding box" that the paragraph of text will fit into.

3. When you release the mouse, you are ready to begin typing text.

4. You can resize the bounding box and change the layout of your text by dragging any of the boxes or handles at the corners and on the sides of a box.

5. You can also use the handles to scale, rotate, or skew the text.

6. When you are finished, commit your changes.

Using the Character Palette

If it is not already open, open the Character palette by choosing Window→ Character.

Many of the options for changing text are available in the Character palette. If you are not sure of the purpose of a particular box, hold your mouse over it for a few seconds and an explanation box will appear.

Following are some key terms in the Character palette:

☆ **Kerning**: Space between letters

☆ **Leading**: Space between lines of text

☆ **Tracking**: Distance across a range of letters

Generally, kerning, leading, and tracking can help increase the readability of your text. Experiment with various settings to see the effect on your text.

Using the Paragraph Palette

The Paragraph palette may already be available as a tab next to your Character palette. Click the Paragraph tab. If it is not available, open the Paragraph palette by choosing Window→Paragraph.

Many options, such as alignment and justification for a paragraph of text, are available in the Paragraph palette. If you are not sure of the purpose of a particular box or button, hold your mouse over it for a few seconds and an explanation box will appear.

◎◎ Using Layers

The Layers feature in Photoshop allows you to place each element of an image in its own distinct space. These spaces, called layers, are stacked on top of each other. By keeping individual elements of an image in separate layers, you can maintain more control of the elements while you are creating the image. In the Layers palette, the topmost layer in the palette is the topmost layer on your image.

In Figure 4.5, the lowest, or Background, layer is white, the red button is the middle layer, and the text is the top layer. Because the elements are on separate layers, you can easily change your mind and make the Background another color, for example. You can also create different sets of text, as shown on the right in Figure 4.5, for use with the same button and Background layers. Figure 4.5 also shows the Character palette and the tab for the Paragraph palette.

Figure 4.5 Button with Two Different Sets of Text

If you had created all these elements on one single layer, it would be difficult to make changes afterward or to create several different buttons from one image.

The Layers feature is available only for images in the Photoshop (PSD) format. When you save images for the Web as JPG or GIF files, the layers are merged or **flattened**, and Photoshop's special features such as Layers are no longer available.

That's another reason you should always go back to your Project PSD file for editing, instead of editing your JPG or GIF file. When you are finished editing your PSD, you can save a new JPG or GIF, replacing the old one.

At the end of this chapter you will learn the steps to make a complex image with many layers. For now, become familiar with the basic techniques for using layers. Create a new image, and experiment with layers of text and shapes as you read through this section on Layers.

Background Layer

Whenever you create a new image with a white or colored background, the bottommost layer is automatically named Background. This layer has some special properties that are useful for advanced techniques. The Background layer cannot be moved.

You can rename the Background layer by double-clicking on it and entering a new name. When you do this, you will make it a normal layer, and it can be moved.

When you create a new image with a transparent background, the bottommost layer is automatically a normal layer and can be moved.

Create two new images, one with a white background and one with a transparent background, and notice the differences between them in the Layers palette.

Adding, Deleting, and Naming Layers

Any time you create a new image, it automatically contains one layer. Whenever you use the Text tool, another new layer is automatically created. You can also create additional empty layers and add content to them. You can name the layers to make their contents easier to identify.

Using one of your new images, try the techniques that follow for adding, deleting, naming, or renaming layers. Refer to Figure 4.6 as you work with these techniques.

Adding a New Layer

To add a new layer, do one of the following:

☆ In the menu at the top of the screen, choose Layer→New→Layer.

or

☆ At the top right of the Layers palette, click the side-pointing triangle to reveal a pop-up menu. Choose New Layer from the menu.

or

☆ Along the bottom bar of the Layers palette, click the Create a New Layer button to the left of the trash can. If you are unsure what all the buttons on the bottom bar mean, hold your mouse over one for a few seconds and an explanation box will appear.

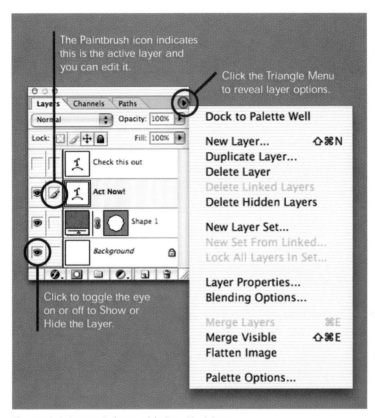

Figure 4.6 Layers Palette with Pop-Up Menu

Deleting a Layer

Your image must always have at least one layer. If you have more than one layer, you can delete layers by doing one of the following:

☆ In the menu at the top of the screen, choose Layer→Delete→Layer.

or

☆ At the top right of the Layers palette, click the side-pointing triangle to reveal a pop-up menu. Choose Delete Layer from the menu.

or

☆ Along the bottom bar of the Layers palette, click the trash can button.

Naming a Layer

When you are working with several layers in an image, it is useful to give them unique names. To name or rename a layer, you can do one of the following:

☆ In the menu at the top of the screen, choose Layer→Layer Properties and type a new name.

or

☆ At the top right of the Layers palette, click the side-pointing triangle to reveal a pop-up menu. Choose Layer Properties from the menu and type a new name.

or

☆ Double-click the layer name in the Layers palette and type a new name.

Selecting Layers

Add a new layer to an image using one of the techniques just listed. Notice that the layer you added is highlighted in color. This means that the layer is selected.

When you are making changes to a layered image, you choose which layer you wish to change before you apply the changes. When a layer is selected, any changes you make apply only to that layer. Only one layer can be selected at a time.

You can select any layer by clicking on it. When a layer is selected, a paintbrush icon appears in the column on the right of the far left column. This means you are ready to edit this layer.

☆ **TIP   Jagged Edges Problem Solved**

Recall that in Chapter Three, when you created a shape, it appeared to have jagged edges. At the time, you had not yet learned about layers.

Now that you have multiple layers in your image, notice that when you select a layer other than a shape layer, the shape layer no longer appears to have jagged edges.

The jagged edges are simply an outline of the shape that appears when that layer is selected.

Showing and Hiding Layers

In the Layers palette, click the eye icon in the far left column of a layer to Show or Hide the layer in your image. When the eye icon is present, the contents of the layer appear in your image. When you click to turn off the eye icon, the contents of the layer are hidden from your image.

If the eye icon is turned off for a particular layer and you save a copy of the image as a GIF or JPG file, the layer will not appear in the GIF or JPG image.

☆ TIP   Showing and Hiding Layers to Create Multiple Buttons

The Show→Hide layer feature is useful when you are experimenting and when you are saving a series of buttons with different sets of text.

For example, you might create a Shape layer for a Web page button and three additional layers, each with different text.

Turn off two of the Text layers and save a GIF file. Then turn on a different Text layer and save another GIF. Repeat. You will now have three GIF files for your Web page, each with the same button shape but with different text on top.

Duplicating Layers

Sometimes it is useful to make a copy of a layer. To duplicate a layer, make sure it is selected. Then choose Layer→Duplicate Layer from the menu at the top of the screen or from the pop-up menu in the Layers palette.

Duplicating layers is especially useful when you want to experiment on an element of your image. If you make a duplicate layer, you can make changes knowing that the original image is intact if you need it later.

Moving Layers

Sometimes it is useful to move layers to change the order of the contents. To move a layer, click, hold, and drag the layer to a new location at the top or bottom of another layer.

Remember that the topmost layer in the Layers palette contains the topmost element of your image. The parts of a layer that do not contain text, color, or a shape show through to the layer below it.

Also, remember that a Background layer cannot be moved, and no other layer can be moved under it. You can Hide the Background layer. You can also Rename a Background layer to make it a normal layer so that it can be moved or another layer moved under it.

Moving the Contents of Layers

Click on your image with the Move tool—in the top right corner of the Toolbox— and move one of the elements. You can move the contents of a layer only when the layer is selected. Moving the contents of a layer allows you to place elements of your image in precise locations.

☆ WARNING   Select the Layer You Want to Change

If you are trying to move or edit your image and nothing happens or the wrong element changes, look at the Layers palette to make sure that the correct layer is selected. If not, click on the layer to select it and try your changes again.

Using Effects and Styles

There are several **effects** that you can apply to a layer. These are called **layer effects**. Together, all the effects that you apply to a particular layer are referred to as the **layer style**. In Chapter Three, you used the Styles palette to apply prebuilt styles to graphic images. Now you will learn to create your own custom styles. You can save your custom styles and use them again later.

You can use effects like Drop Shadow and Bevel and Emboss to add depth and dimension to any layer in your image. You can alter the settings for these effects to achieve a very particular result. A collection of effects and settings is referred to as a Style.

Drop Shadow Effect

To experiment with effects and styles, create an image with a Shape layer and a Text layer.

Adding a Drop Shadow

Select the Text layer. (You are experimenting here with the Text layer, but you can add a drop shadow to any layer.)

☆ In the menu at the top of the screen, choose Layer→Layer Style→Drop Shadow.

or

☆ Along the bottom bar of the Layers palette, click the Add a Layer Style button at the far left. This button is denoted by a dark circle with the letter *f* inside. When the pop-up menu appears, choose Drop Shadow.

Changing the Appearance of the Drop Shadow

When you choose to add the Drop Shadow effect, a Layer Style box appears in which you can adjust several settings. As a beginner, you should concentrate on the settings labeled Structure at the top of the Layer Style box. The Quality settings are best used for advanced techniques. Leave these settings at the default values for now.

Structure Settings in the Drop Shadow Layer Style Box

Refer to Figure 4.7 as you read the following explanations of the settings in the Drop Shadow Layer Style box.

☆ *Blend Mode* and the color chip at the top are advanced settings that you will learn more about in Chapter Eight. Do not adjust these settings now.

☆ *Opacity* specifies the amount of opaqueness of the effect as a percentage. The default is usually 75%. If you move the slider bar or if you type a different number in the box, you change the amount of the effect. At 100%, the effect is completely opaque. At lower percentages, the effect is more transparent and shows through to the layer below it.

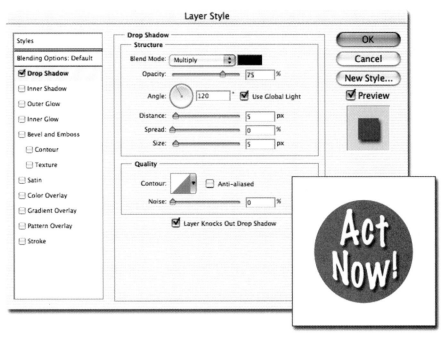

Figure 4.7 Layer Style Box for Drop Shadow Settings

☆ *Angle* specifies the angle in degrees at which the effect will be applied. If you move the angle line within the circle or if you type a different number in the angle box, the effect moves to a different part of the layer.

☆ *Global Light* can be checked on or off. When on, all effects in your current image that have Global Light checked on use the same angle. This means that all the elements in your image appear to have the same source of light casting shadows. If you are unsure about using this adjustment, keep Global Light checked on.

☆ *Distance* is the amount in pixels that the effect will be offset from the layer. You can use the slider bar or type a number directly into the box.

☆ *Spread* modifies the intensity of some of the layer effects. You should probably leave this feature at its default setting.

☆ *Size* is the amount of the effect expressed in pixels. When you increase the size of a drop shadow, the shadow softens and spreads, becoming less defined.

Previewing the Effects

1. While the Layer Style box is open, notice the Preview checkbox in the far right column.

2. When Preview is checked on, you can see the results of the settings you are applying to your image.

3. Be sure to drag your Layer Style box away from your image so that you can see both the image and the Layer Style box at the same time.

4. When you are satisfied with the settings, click OK to exit the Layer Style box and apply the effects.

When you add a drop shadow to the Text layer, notice how the text has taken on more dimension and appears to float above the button below it. Notice that the text layer now has an effect icon in the far right. Next to the icon is a small triangle. Click the triangle to show or hide the list of specific effects that have been applied to the layer.

To see the difference between adding and deleting a particular effect, click the eye icon next to the word Effects in the Text layer. You click the eye to turn the effects on or off. If you have more than one effect on a layer, you can turn individual effects on or off separately.

Bevel and Emboss Effect

The Bevel and Emboss effect is especially useful for adding a three-dimensional look to buttons for your Web site.

Adding a Bevel and Emboss Effect

☆ Select the button layer in your image. (You are experimenting here with the button layer, but you can add Bevel and Emboss to any layer.)

☆ In the menu at the top of the screen, choose Layer→Layer Style→Bevel and Emboss.

or

☆ Along the bottom bar of the Layers palette, click the Add a Layer Style button at the far left. This button is denoted by a dark circle with the letter *f* inside. When the pop-up menu appears, choose Bevel and Emboss.

Changing the Appearance of the Bevel and Emboss Effect

When you choose to add the Bevel and Emboss effect, a Layer Style box appears in which you can adjust several settings. As a beginner, you should concentrate on the settings labeled Structure at the top of the Layer Style box. The Shading settings are best used for advanced techniques. Leave these settings at the default values for now.

Structure Settings in the Bevel and Emboss Layer Style Box

Refer to Figure 4.8 as you read the following explanations of the settings in the Bevel and Emboss Layer Style box.

☆ *Style* includes a pop-up menu in which you can choose among Outer Bevel, Inner Bevel, Emboss, Pillow Emboss, and Stroke Emboss. If Preview is checked on, you can see the result of each of these choices on your image.

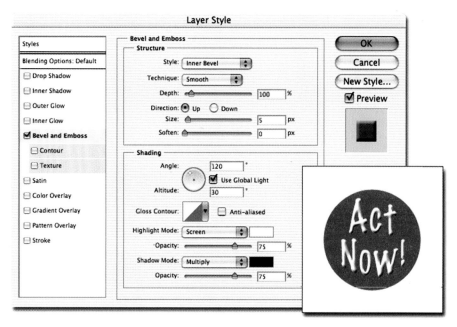

Figure 4.8 Layer Style Box for the Bevel and Emboss Settings

⭐ *Technique* includes a pop-up menu where you can choose among Smooth, Chisel Hard, and Chisel Soft. Preview each of these techniques to see the result on your layer.

⭐ *Depth* changes the appearance of the Bevel and Emboss settings to add more or apply less of the effect on your layer. More depth makes your image appear more three-dimensional. You can change the depth setting by using the slider bar or typing directly into the box at the right.

⭐ *Direction* lets you specify an Up setting or a Down setting. Choose Up to make a button that appears ready to be clicked. Choose Down to make a button that appears to have already been clicked. These are very useful settings when you are making navigation buttons for your Web site.

⭐ *Size* lets you specify the width of the Bevel and Emboss effect. Use a larger size to get a puffier, rounder bevel or emboss. You can change the size setting by using the slider bar or typing directly into the box at the right.

⭐ *Soften* lets you spread the pixels out to soften the edges of the effect. Preview this and any of the above settings to see the result on your layer.

When you are satisfied with the settings, click OK to exit the Layer Style box and apply the effects.

In addition to the Bevel and Emboss effect, you can also add a Drop Shadow to your Shape layer. It will make the button appear to float up off the background. Using effects like Drop Shadow and Bevel and Emboss can make your images stand out and appear more compelling.

Other Effects

When you chose the Drop Shadow or Bevel and Emboss effect for your layer, you probably noticed names of other effects in the list of choices. The number of different effects and the number of settings that can be applied to these effects can be overwhelming for a beginner.

You may wish to concentrate on the Drop Shadow and Bevel and Emboss effects for now and experiment with the other effects later when you have more experience. The Layer Style box will be slightly different for each effect. If you are ever unsure of how or why to change the settings, use the default settings.

☆**TIP**   **Editing Effects**

To change any of the effects you have previously applied to a layer, double-click the name of the effect in the Layer Style list in the layer. This will open the Layer Style box in which you can change any of the settings. Click OK when you are finished to apply the new settings.
   If you are using a prebuilt style for one of your shapes or text, you can use the techniques outlined above to change the appearance of the prebuilt style.

Saving a Custom Style

Remember the Style palette you used in Chapter Three? These prebuilt styles are simply collections of various effects and settings like Drop Shadow and Bevel and Emboss. Now that you've learned to manually use the Drop Shadow and Bevel and Emboss effects, you can make your own preset, or custom, styles.

You might wish to make a **custom style** when you want to apply the same set of effects to several images. For example, use a custom style for all the navigation buttons on your Web site so they will appear uniform.

Follow these steps to save a custom style:

1. If it is not still open, open the shape and text image you created while experimenting with Layer effects. Or create a new image with a Shape and a Text layer.

2. On the Shape layer, double-click the Bevel and Emboss layer style. This will open the Layer Style box. (If you created a new image, add the Bevel and Emboss effect to the Shape layer.)

3. At the top left of the Layer Style box, you will see the word Styles above the list of available effects. Click the word Styles. The box changes to show all the prebuilt styles available.

4. If the Preview box is checked, you will see in the icon below the Preview box a preview of the Bevel and Emboss settings you applied.

5. Above the Preview checkbox, click the New Style button. Another box appears in which you can name your style. For example, type Navigation Buttons in the box next to Name. Be sure to check Include Layer Effects. (Do not check Include Layer Blending Options for now. You will learn more about blending in Chapter Eight.) When you are finished, click OK.

6. You will notice that an icon has been added to the collection of styles. If you hold your mouse over the icon, you will see the name you applied. You can now reuse this style on all the buttons you make for your Web site so that they will appear uniform.

7. To reuse one of your custom styles, open the Styles palette by choosing Window➔Styles at the top of the screen. You will see your custom style along with the other prebuilt styles.

8. Make a new layer at the top of your image, or create a new image. Draw a shape. With the Shape layer selected, click the icon for your custom style. The style will be applied to your Shape layer.

9. When you create a custom style, all the effects you have applied combine to make the custom style.

◎◎ Compositing an Image

You can combine several separate elements to make a **composite** image. Using multiple layers with different elements and effects on each layer, you can create a complex and compelling image. This technique is especially useful when you want to illustrate several ideas in one image.

As you experiment with compositing an image, you will be learning to use more of the tools and features available in Photoshop.

In the composite image shown in Figure 4.9, each element exists on its own layer. Some of the layers have effects. At any time, you can change your mind and change one of the elements without affecting the other elements.

Following is an explanation of the tools and techniques used to make each layer in the figure. Notice the number of layers that make up the complete image. Layer order is important for making elements appear in the correct location.

Create a new image 300 pixels wide by 300 pixels high with a white background. Follow the techniques to create an image similar to the one in Figure 4.9. All the elements needed for this activity are available in the Photoshop program.

1. You created the white Background layer when you created the new image. At any time, you can decide to change the color of the Background layer. But you cannot move a Background layer—it always stays at the bottom—unless you rename it.

Figure 4.9 Composite Image

2. The Sky layer was created with one of Photoshop's Filter tools. On your image, create a new layer above the Background layer and name it Sky. Set the Foreground color in the Toolbox to a bright shade of blue. Set the Background color to white. In the menu at the top of the screen, choose Filter→Render→Clouds. Lower the Opacity setting at the top of the Layers palette to about 75%. This will lighten the layer and make it appear to recede into the white background. If your background color is other than white, this color will be mixed in with the Sky layer when you lower the opacity.

3. The Grass layer was created with the Gradient tool in the Toolbox. On your image, create a new layer above the Sky layer and name it Grass. Set the

Foreground color in the Toolbox to a bright shade of green. Choose the Gradient tool in the Toolbox (about the middle of the right side). Notice the Gradient Fill box on the left side of the Options bar. Click the downward-pointing triangle to reveal various settings for the gradient. Choose the second to top left setting—named Foreground to Transparent. Click your mouse at the bottom middle of your image. Click, hold, and draw upward to the halfway point. Move your mouse a little to the right. Release the mouse. Notice the soft edge where the bright green color begins to blend with the sky. Notice that the angle of the gradient matches the angle you used when you dragged the mouse. Experiment with the Gradient tool by clicking, dragging, and releasing the mouse in short bursts. If you do not like an effect, choose Edit➔Undo and try again.

4. Because the grass is in the foreground of the picture, we want it to stand out and appear closer to the viewer. Adding some texture to the plain green color will help. With the Grass layer selected, choose Filter➔Noise➔Add Noise. Keep the Preview button checked and make adjustments to the settings. When you are finished, click OK.

5. Create a new layer to add the people. Choose a Foreground color in the Toolbox. Select the Custom Shape tool. Click the Options bar to reveal the assortment of custom shapes available. (If there are not very many shapes available in your Custom Shapes box, click the right-pointing triangle menu at the top right of the box. Choose All from the pop-up menu that appears. Additional shapes will be loaded into your Custom Shapes box.) Choose the "people" shape. With your new layer selected, hold, and drag the mouse to draw the people shape in the size you want. Add some shadow and bevel effects to the layer. Do the same procedure to add the bicycle, sun, airplane, cartoon bubble, and flowers layers. Add text to the bubble with the Text tool. (Be sure the Text layer is above the bubble layer.) Add flower stems with a Brush or Pencil tool; put the stems on their own layer. If you make a mistake, use the Eraser tool or choose Edit➔Undo.

6. Create the text that appears at the bottom of the image with the Text tool. The band of color under the text is made with a combination of techniques. Create a new layer under the text. Choose the Marquee Selection tool in the top left of the Toolbox. Click, hold, and drag a box on the layer under the text. Choose a Foreground and Background color. Use the Gradient tool to create a gradient within the selection on the layer under the text. In the Layers palette, with this layer selected, change the Opacity of the layer to about 60%. Be sure there is a good contrast between this layer and the text layer so that the words are readable.

7. Many of the objects in the example have been skewed or distorted with the Transformation tool. Choose Edit➔Transformation➔Skew or Distort in the menu at the top of the screen. These effects can add depth and dimension to elements of the image.

8. Use the Move tool at the top right of the Toolbox when you need to move elements around in the image.

9. Remember that you can change the order of layers by clicking and dragging them.

☆TIP   **Layer Opacity**

Some of the steps used in the composite image in Figure 4.9 require adjustments to **layer opacity**.

A layer's opacity determines the degree to which it shows or hides the contents of the layer below it. At 100% opacity, the content of a layer will completely hide the layer beneath it. If you lower the opacity, more of the layer below will show through.

To set opacity, use the Opacity box at the top right of the Layers palette. Either type a number directly into the box or use the slider to make the setting. Click the side-pointing triangle to the right of the Opacity box to access the slider.

☆ SHORTCUT   **Selecting the Gradient Tool**

To quickly select the Gradient tool, press the Ⓖ key on your keyboard.

◎◎ Saving a Layered Image

The Layers palette and many other tools and techniques are not available unless an image has been saved in the Photoshop PSD file format.

Always use the Save or Save As command to save your original image in the PSD format. Use Save for Web in the File menu at the top of the screen to make a copy of the image in the GIF or JPG format.

Use the GIF or JPG image for your Web site. When you want to change something in the image, edit your PSD file and then save a new GIF or JPG file when you are finished editing.

Review the information about saving your images at the ends of Chapters One, Two, and Three.

Saving a Layered Image

☆ Summary

▷ On the Web, text can be live text or image text.

▷ You can make image text using Photoshop's Text tools.

▷ Use Layers to put each element of an image in its own distinct space.

▷ Use Effects and Styles to add depth and dimension to images.

▷ When you composite an image using different layers for each element, you can always go back and edit a layer without affecting the other layers.

▷ Many of the special features in Photoshop, including Layers, are available only to files saved in the PSD format.

☆ Online References

MSNBC.com—Click one of the Top Stories for an example of a serif font used effectively on the Web for a large body of text.
`http://www.msnbc.com`

Microsoft's Typography site
`http://www.microsoft.com/typography/default.mspx`

Books about type
`http://www.typebooks.org`

1001 Free Fonts
`http://www.1001freefonts.com/`

Download Mac and Windows Fonts
`http://www.fonts.com/`

Top 100 Web sites as ranked by users
`http://www.web100.com`

☆ Review Questions

1. When a user views a Web page, what type of text is embedded in the Web page? What type of text uses fonts from the user's computer?

2. When should you create image text for the Web? When should you create live text for the Web?

3. What type of font, serif or sans serif, is best for large bodies of dense text used on the Web?

4. What are some of the properties of the Text tool that you can set in the Options bar?

5. What is unique about the Background layer?

6. Why would you apply effects and styles to images?

7. Why would you create and save custom styles for your Web buttons?

8. Name an instance where the order of the layers in the Layer palette would be very important.

9. When creating a set of navigation buttons for the Web, why is the Show/Hide Layers feature useful?

10. What special features of Photoshop are available to a PSD file as opposed to a GIF file?

☆ Hands-On Exercises

If you have access to the companion Web site for this book, use those files for the exercises.

1. Use the URL in the "Online References" to see a list of the top 100 Web sites as ranked by users. Go to twenty of the listed Web sites. Notice the use of live text and image text. Keep track of what types of information are used for each type of text.

2. Create two kinds of text, Single Line text and Paragraph text. List the types of content that are best for each type of text.

3. Create a multiple-layered image. Apply effects and styles, and use various tools and filters to create a compelling image. Save the image as a PSD file and as a GIF or JPG for the Web. Open the GIF or JPG file and notice how the layers have been merged or flattened and that individual elements are no longer editable.

4. Create an image with a large body of dense text. Duplicate the Text layer. Choose different font options for each layer. For one layer, choose a serif font. For the other layer, choose a sans serif font. Use Show/Hide Layers, and create a GIF file from each layer. Open the GIF files in separate Web browser windows. Show each file to several people and ask them to compare the readability of the sets of text.

5. Using text and shapes, create a logo for a make-believe company Web site, for example, Grandma's Cookie Factory, Muscle Car Restoration Shop, Adopt a Pet, or Fancy Flowers Landscaping. Be sure the logo is no larger than 60 pixels high and 150 pixels wide.

CHAPTER FIVE

MAKING A WEB ANIMATION

Photoshop's companion application, ImageReady, is a stand-alone application that looks and performs much like Photoshop. ImageReady contains tools for optimizing all your images for the Web and special tools for making animated images. Adding motion to your images creates an interesting dynamic for your Web site. Moving images catch the viewer's eye and hold the viewer's attention. You've probably noticed that many advertisements on Web pages are animated. Sometimes animations are used to illustrate the evolution of an object or idea. Some animations are just plain fun. In this chapter, you will learn how easy it is to make your own Web animation.

Chapter Objectives

★ Learn and apply basic principles of animation

★ Understand another important difference between GIF and JPG images

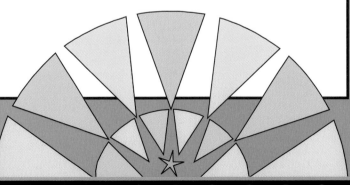

☆ Familiarize yourself with the work area and tools available in ImageReady

☆ Use the animation tools in ImageReady to create an animation

☆ Optimize and save your Web animation

◎◎ Basic Principles of Animation

You've probably enjoyed hundreds of cartoons on television and full-length animated films produced by companies like Disney and Pixar. The basic principles used in those programs are the same ones you will use to make an animation for your Web site.

Walt Disney is often thought of as the Father of Animation. In the early 1920s, he assembled a team of creative people who developed techniques for adding motion to still images. These developments paralleled the development of motion pictures (movies) and eventually television. In all cases, the basic principle is the same. When we view a moving image on a screen, we are actually looking at a series of still pictures that change the image over a period of time. When the pictures change quickly enough, the human eye perceives a fluid motion.

Disney hired talented artists and producers who conceived ideas for stories to be told via animated cartoons. The chief animator would create an image of a character—like Mickey Mouse. The character would be required to move. For example, in a particular scene, Mickey might begin with his arms held up above his head. During the scene, Mickey would lower his arms to his side, raise them again, lower them again, and so on. The chief animator would create the beginning and ending images of the character—one with the arms up and one with the arms down. Then apprentice animators would create the **in-between** images—images with the position of the arms in all the necessary locations to complete the illusion of motion. (Apprentice animators were sometimes referred to as *in-betweeners* or *tweeners*.) Later in this chapter, you will learn to create in-between images, using techniques we call *tweening*.

There are two basic steps for creating a Web animation. First you create a series of images using the Layers feature of Photoshop and/or ImageReady. Then you use special tools in ImageReady to animate the series of images over a period of time. The number of layers you create, the period of time you choose, and the tweening effects you add are important considerations in achieving an optimal animation for the Web.

Animated GIF Images

There are several different types of moving images on the Web, but the most common and the easiest to create is an **animated GIF** image. You learned about the GIF format in Chapters One and Three. Another important feature of the GIF format is that it can contain more than one image and can display the images over a period of time. By using Photoshop/ImageReady and the GIF file format, you can create a Web animation—an animated GIF.

The JPG and PNG formats do not allow for the creation of animated images. Use the GIF format to create a Web animation.

◎◎ Using ImageReady

When you install Photoshop on your computer, the companion application, ImageReady, is also installed. ImageReady is a stand-alone program that can be opened the same way you open any program on your computer. You can also use Photoshop's Jump To button at the bottom of the Toolbox to open or switch to ImageReady. The ImageReady Toolbox also contains a Jump To button for opening or switching back to Photoshop. Figure 5.1 shows the ImageReady work area with the Jump To button at the bottom of the Toolbox.

☆ **TIP**   **Setting Up the Jump To Button**

If your Jump To button does not open the correct application, choose Jump To at the bottom of the File menu. From the fly-out menu, choose Other Graphics Application. In the box that appears, navigate to the icon for the program you wish to open.

ImageReady contains many of the same tools and palettes that are in Photoshop. It also provides many special Web-oriented tools and palettes that are not available in Photoshop. In some cases, similar tools behave slightly differently in ImageReady. As you increase your knowledge and skills, you will find that you switch between the two programs easily.

Like Photoshop, ImageReady includes a Menu bar, an Options bar, a Toolbox, and Palettes. You can show and hide these components as needed while you are working. Use the Window menu at the top of the screen to show or hide the components.

One important difference between Photoshop and ImageReady is that ImageReady includes a palette called Optimize. It is available from the Window menu. Later in this chapter, you will learn to use the settings in the Optimize palette while you create and when you save your image.

Figure 5.1 shows the Optimize palette from ImageReady CS. In earlier versions, the palette looks slightly different, but it contains the same items.

Once you create or open an image in ImageReady, you will notice that tabs appear at the top of your image in the Document window: Original, Optimize, 2-Up, 4-Up. These tabs allow you to view different versions of your image as you create the best possible image for the Web. Notice the tabs at the top of the Document window in Figure 5.1. You will learn more about these tabs later in this chapter.

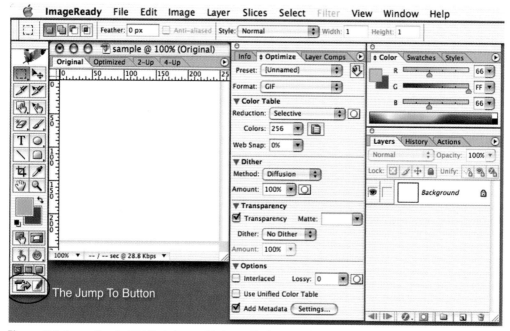

Figure 5.1 ImageReady CS Work Area with Jump To Button, Optimize Palette, and Tabs at Top of Document Window

⊚⊚ Creating a Basic Animation

Always begin with a plan. You may want to review the section in Chapter Three titled "General Information About Graphic Images." With your sketchbook in hand, spend some time surfing the Web and jotting down ideas. Make notes about animations that are impressive, unique, or downright annoying. Note the types of buttons, icons, advertisements, and so on that are animated. Note the animation techniques and sequences. Use separate boxes to denote the multiple screens, and sketch some of your favorite animations. Use colored pencils or markers to add color. You will find that it is much easier to create an animation when you have a plan.

Animated Advertising Banners for the Web

A common use of animation on the Web is for advertising banners. Often, these banners are placed near the top of a Web page and use a common size. They are wide enough to stand out on the page and attract attention but short enough not to take up too much room and obscure the actual content of the page.

Creating a New Web Banner Image

A standard size for advertising banners is 468 pixels wide by 60 pixels high. In the activities in this chapter, you will create an advertising banner for the Web.

1. In ImageReady, create a new image by choosing File→New.

2. At the top of the box that appears, name your image Animation.

3. In the Image Size width and height boxes, type 468 and 60. Or you can click the Custom dropdown box. Notice that presized Web Banner choices are available. Choose the Web Banner (468 × 60) option.

4. Choose White for the Contents of First Layer.

5. Once your new image is open on the desktop, choose File→Save to save your image. ImageReady automatically saves the image as a PSD file.

In this activity, we will make an animated advertisement for a new film. We want to include the name of the film, the name of the creator, and the URL of the Web site where more information is available. We will use text in different sizes and colors for these elements of the animation, and we will also include an image from the film. And we will use special techniques to create the animation. In this example, the name of the film is *Making the Eagle Scream*, and we are using a photograph of an eagle as our image from the film. If you have access to the companion Web site for this book, you can download the image.

If you do not have an eagle handy, you can create one with one of the Painting tools. Figure 5.2 shows the setup for the activity. At the bottom left, you will see an eagle figure that you can draw with a Brush tool if you do not have access to the sample file on the companion Web site.

☆ **WARNING** **Do Not Use the Shape Tools to Create an Image for the Animation Activities**

The activities in this chapter require editing of the eagle image. Editing vector shapes is a complicated procedure requiring use of the Direct Selection tool and advanced knowledge of vector graphics. Use the Painting tools if you are creating an image for these activities.

Be sure your blank Animation image is open on the desktop. Open eagle.psd from the companion Web site, or open the alternate image you are using. The following are two ways to get the eagle (or alternate) image into your blank Animation image:

☆ Click on the eagle image to be sure it is the active document. Then choose Select→All. A selection box, or marching ants, will appear around the image. Then choose Edit→Copy. Click on your blank Animation document and choose Edit→Paste. The eagle will appear in the Animation document as a new layer.

or

☆ A faster technique: Drag the eagle image into your Animation document using the Move tool.

Using the Move Tool

This technique works with almost any layered Photoshop (PSD), not just animated images. Be sure the images are in the RGB Color mode. This technique will not work with images in the Index Color mode.

1. With two image files open side by side, select the Move tool at the top right of the Photoshop or ImageReady Toolbox.

2. Click to select the appropriate layer of the image you wish to move to another location.

3. Using the Move tool, click, hold, and drag the image from its original document to the new document. As you drag the image into the new document, you will notice that a bordered box appears around the new document. This means that you have reached your destination.

4. Let go of the mouse. Notice that the image you moved now appears in the new document as a new layer. You can use the Move tool to place it exactly where you want it.

5. You might need to resize the image to make it fit in the new document. You can use the Edit→Transform tools to scale and orient the image.

Creating Layers for Animation

Remember that animation is really just a series of still images that appear over a period of time. Your first step is to create separate Layers that contain the still images. You can create the layers in either Photoshop or ImageReady.

Once you have prepared the elements of your animation and placed them in separate layers, you will use ImageReady to create **frames** for your animation. The frames of animation allow you to specify a period of time in which the animation takes place. Further, using frames of animation allows you to specify exactly which image appears at exactly which point in time during the animation.

If you have followed along with this activity so far, you already have a Background layer and a layer containing a picture of an eagle or an alternate drawing. For this activity, the picture of the eagle should be 65 pixels wide by 50 pixels high.

If you have to resize your image, use the Transform tool and watch the Info box while you are dragging to get to the correct size. Hold down the Shift key while you drag to constrain the proportions of the image.

Continue to create the elements of your animation by creating three separate text layers for the following three lines:

☆ MAKING THE EAGLE SCREAM
(all caps, font Arial Black, size 14, color red)

☆ *a short film by Stephanie Leigh*
(font Arial, bold italic, size 13, color black)

☆ *www.eaglescream.com* (font Arial, bold italic, size 12, color red)

Of course, you can use other titles and names if you like. Don't worry about where these elements are placed on the image for now. You will arrange them later.

This activity shows the text layers as red and black, but you can use different colors for the text layers. Make sure the colors are bold enough to attract attention. If you are making an advertisement for a company that uses particular colors in its logo, use those colors or complementary ones.

☆**TIP**   **Power of Three**

Notice that in this example, for each line of text, the font size decreases by one. This technique helps carry a viewer's eye from the most important information to the second most important to the third most important information. Designers often use this three-step technique to help the viewer zero in on the three most important elements of an advertisement, brochure cover, Web page, or other informational piece.

Now you have all the elements of your animation. They appear in separate layers in your document. Before you create the actual animation, you must decide which layers will appear in which order over the period of time it takes to play the animation. These choices help you decide the exact location for each of the images in each of the layers.

In our plan for this activity, we want the eagle to fly from the right side of the image to the left. Once the eagle flies, the lines of text will appear on the right, one after another. The lines of text will be stacked and centered.

Now that you know the plan for the animation, you can use the Move tool to arrange the images in each of the layers. Figure 5.2 shows the layers as they will appear at the end of the animation in this example. The eagle is shown here on the left side, or its ending position. It will start out on the right side, though, and we will use animation techniques to make the bird end up on the left. *Put the eagle on the right side to begin.* Arrange the content of your text layers one on top of the other as shown in Figure 5.2.

Creating Frames of Animation

Animation takes place in a series of frames. ImageReady includes an Animation palette that lets you set up the period of time for the animation and specify the images that will appear at certain times. Use the Window→Animation menu to open the Animation palette. A checkmark appears beside the word Animation in the Window Menu when the Animation palette is open.

One of the important aspects of animation is choosing when a particular image is shown or hidden. Remember that in the Layers palette, you can toggle the eye icon in the far left column to Show or Hide a Layer. You will use this technique as you create your animation.

Creating the Frames

1. Organize your layers and the contents of the layers. Toggle the eye off for each of the text layers to Hide them. Leave the Background and eagle layers on. Put the eagle on the right side of the image.

Creating a Basic Animation

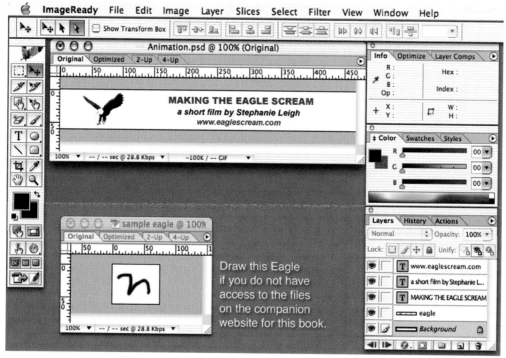

Figure 5.2 Elements of an Animation on Separate Layers and Sample of an Eagle You Can Draw If Needed

2. Open the Animation palette and notice the tabs at the top of the palette. If the Animation tab is not the active window, click the Animation tab at the top of the palette.

3. Notice that the first frame of animation is already made. It shows the white background and the eagle layers. All the layers that show in the Layers palette (eye on) will show in the frame of animation. If any of the text layers are showing now, click to toggle the eye off to Hide the text layers for now.

4. In Figure 5.3, there are two frames in the Animation palette. The second frame contains exactly the same content as the first frame. You create additional animation frames by clicking the Duplicate Current Frame button at the bottom of the Animation palette.

5. Once a new frame is created, you can change which layers Show or Hide, thus changing the contents of the frame. Be sure the appropriate frame of animation is selected, then Show or Hide appropriate layers.

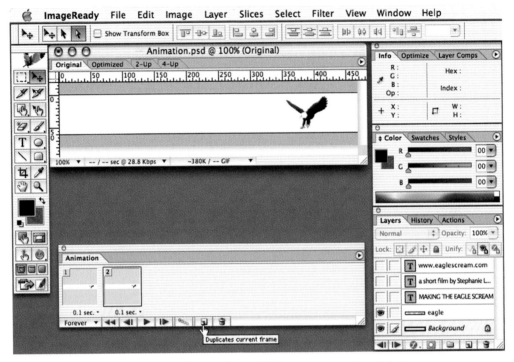

Figure 5.3 Image, Layers Palette with Text Layers Hidden, and Animation Palette with Two Frames of Animation

☆ **TIP**   **Selecting Frames**

Click once on a frame to select it. In Figure 5.3, notice that the second frame is highlighted, indicating that it is selected. To select more than one frame, hold down the ⌐Control⌐ key (Windows) or the Command ⌐⌘⌐ key (Mac) while you click on the frames.

Making the Eagle Fly

1. Make sure the second frame of animation is selected in the Animation palette. In the Layer palette, click to select the eagle layer.

2. Use the Move tool to move the eagle to the far left side of the image. Hold down the ⌐Shift⌐ key while you move the eagle to constrain the horizontal position.

3. In the Animation palette, hold down the ⌐Control⌐ (Command ⌐⌘⌐) key to select both frames 1 and 2.

4. Notice the sideways-pointing triangle at the top right of the Animation palette. Click it to reveal the Animation palette menu. Choose Tween.

5. In the box that appears, choose Tween with Selection from the dropdown menu.

6. Type 2 in the Frames To Add box.

7. In the Parameters section, click to *deselect* the Opacity box. Click OK.

8. In the Animation palette, notice that two new frames have been added between your original frames.

9. Click the Play button at the bottom of the Animation palette, and watch the eagle fly.

10. Click the Stop button to stop the animation. Use the Rewind and Step Backward and Step Forward buttons to view the animation one frame at a time.

It's a very simple animation, but it should give you a good idea of how animation works.

Two Ways to Add More Tweened Frames

There are two things you might want to do to make the animation more fluid: add more tweened frames and/or adjust the period of time in which the animation takes place.

1. You can start over and use a larger number in the Frames To Add box in the Animation palette menu. This method will automatically create more tweened frames.

2. You can use the Duplicate Current Frame button to create more frames. Then, using the Layer palette, you can use the Move tool to make slight changes to the location of the eagle for each frame.

3. If you need to delete a frame of animation, click once on it to select it, and then click the trash can icon at the bottom of the Animation palette.

4. Be careful not to add too many tweened frames for an animated GIF. A large number of frames will increase the file size of your GIF, thus increasing the download time on the Web.

You've no doubt noticed that the eagle did not magically flap its wings during flight. Using the Tween menu does not automatically alter the shape of your original image. In this example, tweening created new frames with the image in new locations, thus moving the image from one place to the next. Later in this chapter, you'll learn advanced techniques to make the eagle flap its wings.

In the Parameters box in the Tween menu, you can choose to tween the Position, the Opacity, and/or the Layer Effects (such as Drop Shadow settings). You can experiment with different choices in the Tween menu to see the results. Tweening automatically creates new frames with the appropriate interim frame edits already made. You could do this manually, but using the Tween command is much faster.

As you experiment, you will see that you can use many different techniques. For example, you can use Opacity (which we turned off for this activity) to make an animated image appear to fade in or fade out. You might also want to Tween with size. Make a duplicate layer of an image and use the Transform tools to make the duplicate larger or smaller. Then use the Tween command to create additional frames of animation that will produce a growing or shrinking effect. The possibilities are endless.

Timing the Animation

Now you will adjust the period of time for the animation. First add the text layers to your animation by creating duplicate frames. Click to select the last frame of animation. Then click the Duplicate Current Frame button.

1. Leave the eagle layer showing and click to Show the layer containing the title of the film.

2. Duplicate another frame and Show the text layer that includes the name of the creator.

3. Duplicate another frame and Show the text layer that includes the Web address.

4. Now you are ready to add timing to your animation.

When you click the Play button to view your animation, each frame appears one right after another with no delay in between. Depending on the effect you are trying to achieve, the animation may be moving too quickly.

Figure 5.4 shows that delay times have been added to each frame. The pop-up menu at the bottom of each frame lets you choose an amount of time in fractions of seconds or full seconds. You can also choose Other and type a specific number of seconds.

There is also a pop-up menu at the bottom left corner of the Animation Palette that lets you Select Looping Options. You can choose to have your animation play continuously without ever stopping by choosing Forever in this menu. Or you can choose to have the animation play once and stop by choosing Once. There is also an Other selection in which you can type a specific number of times for the animation to play.

You should experiment to get your animation just right. Remember that the combination of number of frames and the timing for each frame is the recipe for success.

If you have important information such as a name or Web URL that you want the viewer to remember, you should add more delay for those frames. If you want motion to appear more fluid, add more frames and get the timing just right for each frame.

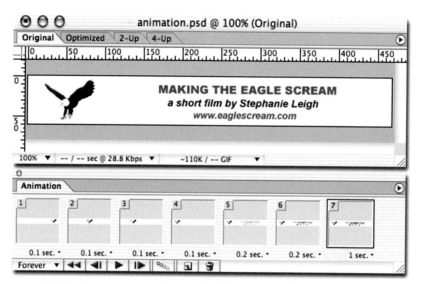

Figure 5.4 Animation Palette Showing the Frames of Animation and the Timing for Each Frame

☆**WARNING** **Test Your Animation on the Web**

Once you add your animation to an actual Web site, you will see how connection speeds on different computers affect your animation. Slow connection speeds will slow your animation. Fast connections may make your animation run too fast. Put your animation on a Web site and test it on several computers. If it does not play the way you intended, go back and modify the animation.

In the research you did at the beginning of this chapter, you probably noticed several animations on the Internet that became annoying when they were repeated endlessly. Keep this in mind as you create your animation. Sometimes playing an animation once or only a few times can have a more powerful impact on the viewer.

Once you put your animation on a Web page, you can add a hyperlink. When the viewer clicks on the animation, they will link to a new Web page. You will learn how to make hyperlinks later in this book.

◎◎ Creating a Complex Animation

Software programs like Flash are especially suited for making complex Web animations. But you can use Photoshop and ImageReady to make interesting animations as well. (In Photoshop CS and later versions, you can create an ImageReady animation and export it as a Flash file for the Web. See Chapter Eight for more information.)

The basic animation you created in the earlier activity will certainly do the job of catching the viewer's attention. But you probably still want that eagle's wings to flap while it flies. Making the parts of an object change during the animation requires more time and skill. The more you know about drawing, the better you will be at creating complex animations.

Animation in Place

In this activity, we want to make the eagle's wings change position while the eagle is moving across the screen. We can do so using the Layers, Selection, Copy→Paste, and Transform tools in Photoshop or ImageReady. First, we will make the wings flap. This is called **animation in place**. To change the parts of an object, follow these steps:

1. Use File→New to create a new blank Web banner image with a white background.

2. Add a layer with the eagle by using the Move tool or the Copy→Paste commands.

3. Select the eagle layer and make a duplicate of it. Use the Layer menu at the top of the screen or the triangle menu at the top right of the Layers palette to make the duplicate. Name this layer Body Only.

4. Use the Zoom tool to magnify the eagle in the new layer so that you can make precise selections while you change the wing positions.

5. Use the Lasso tool to encircle one of the wings and let go of the mouse. A flashing selection will appear as shown in Figure 5.5. If you did not make a precise selection, choose Select→Deselect from the Menu at the top of the screen and try again.

Figure 5.5 Part of the Object Selected and Then Transformed

6. Choose Edit➔Cut from the menu at the top of the screen. The wing you selected will disappear.

7. Create a new layer and choose Edit➔Paste. The wing you selected now appears alone on its own layer. Use the Move tool to move the wing on top of the original wing.

8. Choose Edit➔Transform➔Rotate from the menu at the top of the screen. Near the top right corner of the bounding box that appears, click, hold, and drag outside the small corner box. Drag to make the wing position go down about 45 degrees. To complete the transformation, click the Commit button in the Options bar or click the Move tool.

9. Use the Move tool to position the wing next to the eagle's body. You may have a problem with layer order. In this example, the new wing position obscures part of the eagle's head. To correct the problem, drag the new wing layer down below the layer with the original eagle.

10. Be sure to name your layers by choosing Layer➔Layer Options from the menu at the top of the screen or from the triangle menu on the Layers palette. This will help you keep track of the new wings and wing positions.

11. Duplicate your newest layer. Rename it, transform it another 45 degrees, and move it into the correct position. Do the same to create a third wing position.

12. Click to select the Body Only layer and apply the same techniques to the other wing: use the Lasso tool to select and Edit➔Cut the other wing.

13. Create a new layer and choose Edit➔Paste. Rename the layer. Transform the position of the wing. Use the Move tool to position the wing as needed.

14. Create two more wing layers by duplicating the wings-only layers. Transform the positions another 45 degrees for each.

15. Now you are ready to make frames of animation using the Animation palette. Start with only the original eagle layer showing. Make a duplicate frame and turn layers on and off to show the second position for each wing. Make another duplicate frame and show the third wing positions. For the duplicate frames, use the Body Only layer rather than the original eagle layer.

16. Play your animation and watch the eagle flap its wings. Adjust the timing to get the effect you want.

Animation in Place and Along a Path

In the basic animation activity you completed first in this chapter, the eagle flew but did not flap its wings. We call the movement **animation along a path**. In the complex animation activity you just began, the eagle is flapping its wings but not flying. We call this movement **animation in place**.

To make the eagle flap *and* fly, you can combine the two types of animation To do so, you will use more advanced techniques, including Linked Layers and Layer

Sets. These techniques can be used with any Photoshop/ImageReady images, not just animations.

The following steps explain how to combine place and path animation:

1. Open the animation-in-place (Animation) document you created previously.

2. Remember that you can edit any frame of your animation by clicking to select the frame in the Animation palette and then showing, hiding, or moving the contents in the layers in the Layer palette. In this activity, you will mess up one of the frames of your animation, but you can fix it later by editing the frame.

3. Notice the box to the right of the eye icon in each layer. This is the Link box. When a layer has been linked, a chain icon appears in this box. When you link layers, you can move, duplicate, or change their contents all at the same time.

4. Select the last frame of your animation. Select the original eagle layer in the Layers palette. Click the Link box for each of the other layers except for the Background layer. Now all the layers (except the Background layer) are linked together.

5. *ImageReady 7:* From the menu at the top of the screen or from the triangle menu at the top right of the Layers palette, choose New→Layer Set From Linked. When you perform this command in Photoshop or in ImageReady, all the linked layers are placed inside a folder in a new layer called a Layer Set. A downward-pointing triangle appears to the left of the Layer Set name. Click it to collapse or reveal the contents of the Layer Set.

6. *ImageReady CS:* This version of the program uses Layer Sets and Linking a bit differently. Use the triangle menu to create a New Layer Set. Then link your other layers as explained in step 4. Use the triangle menu to Select Link Layers. Then, move the group of linked layers into the Layer Set folder.

7. Click the triangle near the Layer Set name to collapse the contents of the Layer Set. With the Layer Set layer selected, use the Duplicate Layer Set command to make a copy of the Layer Set.

8. Duplicate more Layer Sets. The more Layer Sets you make, the more fluid your animation will be. However, if you are a beginner, sometimes it is easier to work with only two or three Layer Sets.

9. Now duplicate the last frame of your original animation. With this frame selected, hide the first Layer Set and show the second Layer Set. With the second Layer Set selected (the layer with the folder icon, not one of the linked layers within), use the Move tool to move the eagle toward the center of the image. Then show and hide the appropriate linked layers to change the position of the wings.

10. Look at your Animation palette. If one of the frames of your animation does not contain the correct images, edit it by hiding or showing the correct layers and Layer Sets in the Layer palette.

11. Duplicate new frames of animation, and hide and show appropriate Layer Sets and linked layers to change the position of the eagle and wings.

12. Figure 5.6 shows a complex animation with eight frames of animation and six Layer Sets. In the Animation palette, you can see the different positions of the eagle and the different positions of the wings in each frame. You can make as many frames and layers as you like to create a fluid animation.

13. For an even more complex animation, you might also use the Tween command to automatically add tweened frames of animation.

14. As you create and test your complex animation, you may want to set the Looping Option to Once. You can also use the Step Forward and Step Backward buttons to view the animation one frame at a time. When you see an error, stop and edit the frame.

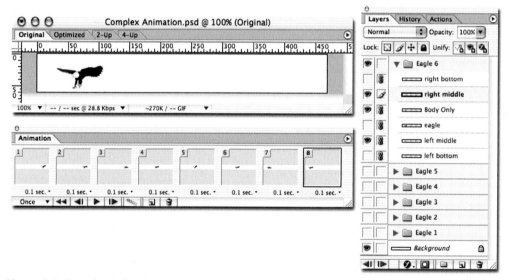

Figure 5.6 Complex Animation

☆**TIP   Using Duplicate Layers**

If you are unsure how you wish to edit a layer or want to experiment without fear of ruining your original, make a duplicate copy of the layer. If things don't work out, you can always discard the duplicate layer and still have the original layer intact.

☆ **SHORTCUT   Transform Tool**

With the desired layer selected, press (Control) (Windows) or Command (⌘) (Mac) and the letter T on the keyboard. A bounding box will surround the object in the layer. Use the small boxes in the corners to click, drag, and scale the object. Click, hold, and drag outside the small boxes in the corners to rotate the object.

☆ **SHORTCUT   Renaming a Layer**

You can double-click the name of a layer to rename it. Don't forget to press the (Enter) or (Return) key to complete the process.

◎◎ Optimizing and Saving Your Animation for the Web

☆**WARNING   Use the GIF File Format for Animations**

To create an animation in ImageReady, you must be sure that the image is in the GIF format. Animations will not work in the JPG or PNG formats.

The Optimize tools in ImageReady work in similar ways to the Save for Web box in Photoshop. The Optimize palette and the tabs at the top of your image are tools for processing your image to make it the best it can be for the Web. For animations, ImageReady also includes a special Optimize Animation command in the Animation palette menu.

Optimize Animation Menu Command

Choose Optimize Animation from the Animation palette menu. By default, the Bounding Box and Redundant Pixel Removal options are checked on. Bounding Box means that areas of the frame that change from one frame to the next will be processed in an optimal manner. Redundant Pixel Removal is a processing method that deals with images that have transparent areas. Leave both these options checked on to be assured that your animation will be processed correctly.

Optimize Palette

Choose Window→Optimize to open the Optimize palette. Click on one of the active layers in one of the frames of your animation. Make sure that GIF is selected from the dropdown box at the top of the Optimize palette.

Ideally, you should check the Optimize palette whenever you create a new layer when using ImageReady. Shapes, graphics, and animated images are best saved as GIF images. Photographic images should be saved as JPG images. (The PNG format is becoming popular on the Web, but it is still not widely supported and is not covered in this book.)

The Optimize palette contains the same types of settings and options that you learned in the Save for Web section of Chapter Three. You can review that information to refresh your memory.

Tabs at the Top of the Document Window

In ImageReady, the tabs at the top of your image are similar to the Preview options available in Photoshop's Save for Web box. You can choose to see your original image or the optimized image based on the settings you have chosen. You can also choose the 2-Up and 4-Up tabs. When you choose the 2-Up tab, you will see your original image in one panel and your optimized image in the other panel. The 4-Up tab lets you see your original image and three different options for your optimized image.

The 2-Up views are used in the figures in this book to assure that images are large enough so that details can be seen on the printed pages. However, you may wish to use the 4-Up tab so that you can experiment with three different sets of image settings before you choose the one you wish to finally save. Change the settings for each of the images and notice the differences in file size, download time, visual quality, and so on.

Figure 5.7 shows the complex animation we made in this activity with the 2-Up tab selected. One of the layers used in the animation is selected, and the Optimize palette shows that it will be processed as a GIF image.

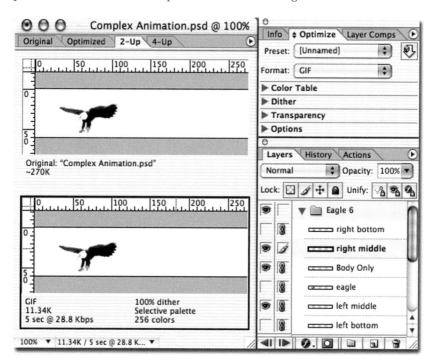

Figure 5.7 2-Up Tab in the Document Window, Optimize Palette, and Highlighted Layer in the Layers Palette

☆**TIP**   **Moving Around the Image in the 2-Up and 4-Up Settings**

Sometimes you do not have enough room on the screen to show your entire image
when you use the 2-Up and 4-Up tabs in the document window. Choose the Hand tool
from the Toolbox, then click, hold, and drag on the image to move to another area of the image.

Saving Your Animation

When you choose Save from the File menu, you are saving your original layered
ImageReady file. It will be saved in the PSD format by default. By saving this file,
you will always be able to go back later and edit your animation. Be sure to Save
your original layered ImageReady file by choosing File➔Save.

The File menu in ImageReady also contains additional Save commands that
allow you to save a copy of your image in the GIF or JPG formats. You will use the
GIF format for your animation:

1. Choose Save Optimized from the File Menu.

2. Select the destination for your image and check the name. Because this image
   will be used on the Web, do not use spaces or special characters in the name.

3. In the Format dropdown menu, choose Images Only. You will learn more
   about the other settings later in this book.

4. In the Settings dropdown menu, choose Other. When you choose Other, the
   Output Settings box appears. Leave the default settings, with one exception: in
   the Optimized Files section, click to be sure the Put Images in Folder and Copy
   Background are unchecked.

5. Click OK to save your animated GIF.

You will learn more about the advanced settings available with the Save
Optimized command later in this book.

Now you are ready to put the animated GIF image on a Web page, where it will
be viewed in a browser. Remember that download time is always something to consider when making images for the Web. Avoid creating complex animations that
take a long time to download over slow Internet connections. Experiment with several versions of your animations to find the best-looking image with the fastest
download time.

☆ Summary

▷ An animation is basically a series of still images that appear over a period of time.

▷ Although you can use either program to create the original layered images, use ImageReady, not Photoshop, to create the final animation.

▷ Use layers to create the individual elements of the animation. Use frames to create the period of time for the animation. Hide and Show layers in separate frames to create the effect of movement.

▷ Tweening is a way to have ImageReady automatically create frames of animation. You can also make tweened frames yourself.

▷ Carefully timing the frames of animation will make the animation play smoothly.

▷ Two types of animation are animation in place and animation along a path. You can combine these types of animation to create a complex animation.

▷ ImageReady animations must always be saved as GIF files.

☆ Online References

About.com's Animation Fundamentals
`http://animation.about.com/library/weekly/aa021100a.htm`

Hotwired's WebMonkey Animation Tutorial
`http://hotwired.lycos.com/webmonkey/98/32/`
`index0a.html?tw=multimedia`

Pixar Studios *How We Do It*
`http://www.pixar.com/howwedoit/index.html`

Kingston Museum, Eadweard Muybridge's Running Horse
`http://213.48.46.171/museum/muybridge/`

Character Animation: Principles and Practice
`http://www.comet-cartoons.com/toons/3ddocs/charanim/`

WebReference—The Art of Animation
`http://webreference.com/dlab/9904/principles.html`

☆ Review Questions

1. What are the two primary steps for creating an animation in ImageReady?

2. What is the difference between a layer and a frame?

3. Why would you add tweened frames to an animation?

4. Describe an animation in place.

5. Describe an animation along a path.

6. In what file format must an ImageReady animation be saved?

☆ Hands-On Exercises

If you have access to the companion Web site for this book, use those files for the exercises.

1. Use ImageReady and the Brush tool to draw a simple stick figure. Using the techniques from this chapter, make the arms and legs appear to move. For example, use the Lasso tool to select an arm. Copy the selection, paste it in a new layer, and transform the position of the arm. Use the same techniques to make additional layers with the arms and legs in different positions.

2. Continue with the same document. Create frames of animation, showing and hiding different layers at different points in time.

3. Add some tweened frames, using the triangle menu in the Animation palette.

4. Add timing to the animation.

5. Save your animation as a GIF file and test it in a Web browser by dragging the Animated GIF file into a browser window.

CHAPTER SIX

DESIGNING A WEB PAGE

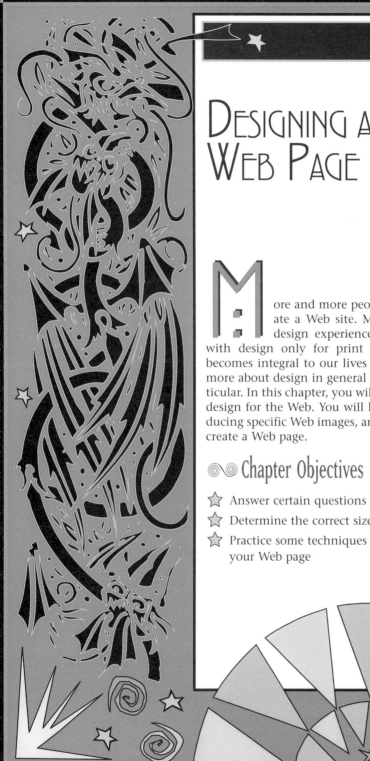

More and more people are finding a reason to create a Web site. Most of them have little or no design experience. Some may have experience with design only for print publications. As the Internet becomes integral to our lives and work, we should all learn more about design in general and design for the Web in particular. In this chapter, you will learn some basic principles of design for the Web. You will learn some techniques for producing specific Web images, and you will begin to design and create a Web page.

⊚⊚ Chapter Objectives

☆ Answer certain questions before you begin your design

☆ Determine the correct size for your Web page

☆ Practice some techniques for deciding on the design of your Web page

☆ Produce background images and simple Rollover images

☆ Learn the importance of getting feedback on your design

◎◎ Web Design Basics

Consider the many functions of a Web site. It is used to display information. It contains navigation so that users can find their way around. It presents choices to the users. Sometimes it allows for user interaction. In all cases, it communicates. And it is out there for the world to see. Designing Web pages that are both functional and attractive is no easy task. Get your sketchbook out and start now.

You should answer many questions before you begin to design:

☆ Who is my audience?

☆ What do I want them to do?

☆ What are the categories of information to be displayed?

☆ How much existing material do I already have?

☆ How much material will I need to obtain?

☆ What will be an appropriate *look and feel* for the site?

☆ What ideas have I seen on the Web that I would like to emulate?

☆ How much experience do I have?

Novice designers should approach Web design with these things in mind:

☆ Keep it simple. Don't bite off more than you have the experience to chew.

☆ Symbols and metaphors are keys to interesting design. Repeat certain elements to create a visual theme that exists over multiple pages.

☆ Alignment and balance of the elements on a page are very important to the overall look.

☆ Contrast will make things stand out.

☆ *White space* is good. Try to have plenty of blank areas on your page—especially around large blocks of text. Novice designers often try to cram images and text into every part of the page, leaving the viewer's eye with no relief and no idea where to look first.

☆ Less is more. Web users quickly scan the contents of a page. Readability of the text is extremely important.

☆ Think deep. Keep your users clicking for more, rather than giving them everything on one page.

☆ One good picture really is worth a thousand words.

The basic components of a Web page are **text**, **links**, and **images**. Often, the first time a designer creates a Web site, there is more text than images available for content. That's OK—having lots of text means that you can create several pages and link them together with navigation buttons.

Images for Web pages usually take two forms—pictures that illustrate ideas and people mentioned in the text and buttons that allow for navigation throughout the site. In this chapter, you will learn design techniques for combining text, navigation, and images to create a Web page.

Following are the first steps to take in creating a Web page or Web site:

1. *Start with a plan.* After answering the questions listed at the beginning of the chapter, determine the number of pages you will have, and sketch a flowchart that illustrates the links between pages like the one shown in Figure 6.1. Once you have done so, you will have a good idea of what your navigation menu should include. Try to condense the names of the menu items to one or two words each. Consider how often you want to update the site. For example, don't create an elaborate "What's New" section if you won't have time to keep the material fresh.

2. *Create a Color Guide* for your site (see Chapter One). For novice designers, fewer colors are better. You will need to consider a color scheme that includes backgrounds, text, buttons, and links. If you have a logo, a picture, or another element with existing important colors, use those or a complementary scheme. Color and the contrast between colors will help create the look and feel for your site. (White can be considered a color.) Be consistent with the color scheme throughout the pages of your Web site.

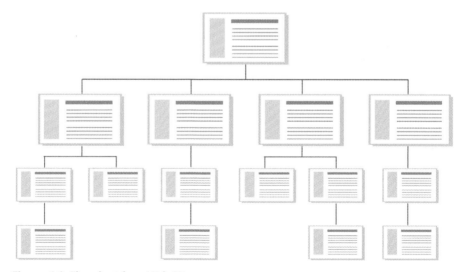

Figure 6.1 Flowchart for a Web Site

3. *Consider the fonts* you will use. (See Chapter Four for important details about text on the Web.) Determine which items of text will be image text and which will be live text. For live text, stick with fonts you know almost every computer contains. Times New Roman, Arial, and Verdana are fonts often used for live text on the Web because nearly every user's computer contains these fonts. For image text, find the perfect font to express your ideas and set a tone for the site.

4. *Organize your files*. Make a project folder where you keep all the materials you gather for the Web site. Keep original images in your Master Originals folder, and put copies in your Project folder. Edit your copies, not your originals. (See Chapter One, especially "Strategy for Saving Your Images.")

5. *Consider the visual layout* of your home page and inside pages. Design will draw users to and through your Web site, so make plenty of sketches before you decide which layout you will use. Make small **thumbnail sketches**, using boxes and shapes to denote the content. When a particular layout appeals to you, make a larger sketch and fill in some actual content to see how it will work. If you don't have a sketchbook, use an 8½-by-11-inch sheet of paper, turned horizontally. Computer screens are wider than they are tall, and the proportions of one screen of information are similar to those of a regular sheet of paper turned horizontally.

6. *Determine the physical size of your Web pages*. Page sizing can be difficult for a Web designer because technology is always changing and because different users have different computers, monitors, and browsers. At the time of this writing, most computer monitors use a size—or resolution—of at least 800 pixels wide by 600 pixels high. Older, smaller monitors use 640 pixels wide by 480 pixels high. Large monitors use 1024 pixels by 768 pixels or even larger displays. Choose a size for your page that works best for your content and for your intended audience.

☆TIP   **A Good Reason for Watching Television**

Like a computer monitor, a TV screen is also a wider-than-tall format. With your sketchbook handy, watch television to get ideas for designing your Web page layout. In particular, notice cable TV news channels like CNN, MSNBC, and Fox News. They use a lot of images and text on the screen, and sometimes the content looks like a Web page. (Turn the sound off so you can concentrate on design.)

◎◎ Using Photoshop and ImageReady to Design a Web Page

Some Web page creators approach the design of a page by starting with hand-coded HTML or a Web editing program like Adobe Go Live, Macromedia Dreamweaver, or Microsoft Front Page. They turn to Photoshop whenever they need to create an image for the page and then return to HTML or the editing program. Of course, these creators will find much useful information about creating and editing images in this book.

Because this is a book about Photoshop/ImageReady, it takes a slightly different approach. If you create your Web page by starting with Photoshop, you will be able to concentrate on the overall design, color, and layout without getting too bogged down in the particulars of HTML techniques. You can then take parts of your design or even the entire design and use it with HTML or a Web editing program. The result is often a more pleasing and coherent overall design than if you had started with HTML or a Web editor.

Whether you start with a Web editor or with Photoshop, eventually you will get to the same place. A functional and attractive Web page is a unique document. You will have to make HTML-based changes to accommodate design needs, and you will have to make design changes to accommodate HTML needs.

You can use either Photoshop or ImageReady to begin the design for your Web page. At a certain point, you will use ImageReady exclusively in order to take advantage of special Web tools.

With Photoshop, you can do the following:

☆ Create a blank page.

☆ Design a Web page by combining text, images, and links.

☆ Divide—or **slice**—the page into smaller sections for output as Web page images.

☆ Optimize the images for the Web.

☆ Save the page and/or slices from the page. You can choose to save individual elements alone for use with a Web editor, or you can choose to save a complete HTML file along with your images.

With ImageReady, you can do all of the above PLUS the following:

☆ Use additional slicing, optimizing, and programming tools

☆ Create and preview animations and Rollover behaviors.

◎◎ Designing a Web Page

Open Photoshop. You are ready to begin with a new, blank canvas, and you should have a general idea of what the physical size of your page will be.

☆ **TIP**   **Use Pixels, Not Inches**

If necessary, change the Preferences for Units and Rulers in the Edit menu to choose Pixels as your Unit of Measurement. Use the View menu to Show Rulers.

Creating a New Document to Match the Size of Your Web Page

Use File→New to create a new document with a white background. Be sure that the Color Mode is RGB and the resolution is 72 pixels per inch.

If you are unsure what size to use, assume that your viewers will have monitors set at 800 pixels wide by 600 pixels tall. The size of your page will be based on this assumption, but remember that the browser window itself takes up space at the top and sides. *This means that the available space for one screen of information is only about 760 pixels wide by 420 pixels high.* Many home pages use exactly this size so that the viewer does not have to scroll at all. Sometimes this type of wide and short home page is called a **splash screen**.

Viewers with a monitor resolution of 1024 by 768 can see the full content of a browser window that is up to 600 pixels high without scrolling. The available width goes up to 950 pixels.

If you have a lot of content for the home page and you don't think users will mind if they have to scroll, use a larger height. If you are creating an inside page, it will probably be taller as well.

Because technology is always changing, you should stay abreast of trends. The following URL will keep you informed about the most current information on average monitor sizes:

http://www.w3schools.com/browsers/browsers_stats.asp

Visually Dividing the Design Area into Rows and Columns

Use all the information presented so far to determine a width and height for your practice Web page. *If you cannot decide, use 760 pixels wide by 600 pixels high.* These dimensions will give you enough room to rough out your design.

You've probably used a word processor to create a **table** that has columns and rows. The areas created by the intersection of rows and columns are called **cells**. Visually dividing any design surface into rows and columns is useful for general design and is very important for Web design. If you use a Web editing program to create a Web page, you will probably use tables to control the layout of your design.

To begin your design, imagine—or draw in your sketchbook—a table with three rows and three columns (Figure 6.2). Imagine that your Web page is divided into the same columns and rows.

As a Web designer, one of the obstacles you encounter is that you do not know what type of monitor the viewer is using. This means that you do not really know where the right side of a browser window will actually be. Also, because Web pages can scroll down endlessly, you have a lot of flexibility with the actual height of your page. Regardless of their monitor sizes, users may scrunch up the browser windows from the right and from the bottom. It is always a challenge to consider how to treat the right side and the bottom of a Web page design.

In Figure 6.2, notice the light gray portions of the table. *This is the area in which you should place your most important information.* For example, if you have a logo, place it in the top left corner.

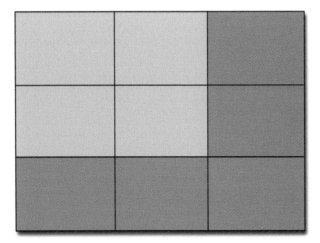

Figure 6.2 Table with Three Rows and Three Columns

To help visually divide your document, you can use the Guide tool, available in both Photoshop and ImageReady.

1. Be sure that you have rulers turned on by choosing Rulers in the View menu.

2. Choose the Move tool from the Toolbox.

3. Inside one of the rulers at the top or left side of your document, click, hold, and drag out onto the canvas. Let go of the mouse.

4. Notice that a thin blue line appears. This is a **guide**. You can use the Move tool to move it to another location. You can watch the Info Window to see exactly where you are placing the guide. You can create as many vertical or horizontal guides as you wish.

5. Guides are for use only within Photoshop/ImageReady. They will not appear when you print the document or when you save your document as an image file.

Using Symbols and Metaphors to Help Determine Your Design

Most graphic designers spend a lot of time considering ways to express ideas by using symbolic imagery and metaphor. For example, use of a country's flag and the colors in the flag might evoke the idea of national pride in a "Don't Forget to Vote" Web site. A Web site for schoolchildren might use bright yellow school buses as the imagery for menu items. A community organization Web site might use a village theme.

Novice Web designers may feel comfortable using design layouts that evoke the idea of the printed page—for example, a newspaper, magazine, or book. These layouts use columns and rows and are useful for designing many Web pages.

Newspapers use up to six or seven columns. Magazines use two or three columns. Books use one or two columns. Consider how your Web page or site might use one or more of these setups. For good examples of Web pages that have a lot of text content, look at sites like MSNBC.com and Salon.com. Their news stories are excellent examples of *text-heavy* Web pages that are both easy on the eyes and quite readable on the screen.

The first time you create a Web page, it is most likely to be a personal page rather than a page for a commercial business. Personal pages make great first-time Web sites because you are familiar with the topic and you probably already have pictures you can use. You can also get valuable feedback from your family and friends in a supportive atmosphere.

Figure 6.3 shows a home page created by a writer. Naturally, he has a lot of text that will be used on the Web site. Let's examine some of the key aspects of this design:

☆ The top two-thirds of this page contains two columns, with text beginning in the upper left where it will be seen first in small browser windows. The text is presented in three sizes, with the largest on top. The quotation used as a headline at the top of the page is a **grabber**—designed to attract the viewer's attention. The decreasing sizes of text below the headline provide contrast and lead the viewer's eye down through the rest of the content. All the text is aligned at the left, giving a strong left edge to the top part of the page. The quotation at the top and the subhead beneath are both in a large size of the Times font (a serif font). A sans serif font, Verdana, is used for the body text. See Chapter Four for more information about choosing fonts for Web text.

☆ The use of a large picture on the right, next to the column of text, evokes the idea of a magazine. Sometimes, one good picture—well placed—is more compelling than several smaller pictures. If the viewer has a slow Internet connection speed and the picture takes a few seconds to load, at least it is off to the right, and the viewer can begin reading the text immediately. In Chapter Seven, you will learn how to Slice large images to improve download time.

☆ Hold this book away from you, and squint your eyes while you look at Figure 6.3. Notice how the white space becomes a part of the design. Always use plenty of white space at the sides of a block of text to increase readability. The white space around the picture, especially at the bottom, helps relieve the eye as it views the large amount of content.

☆ Consider the balance in this design. The dark color at the bottom of the page balances the large amount of white at the top. The large photo balances the large block of text. The small bar of color at the top separates the page from the Web browser window and repeats the colors from the bottom of the page.

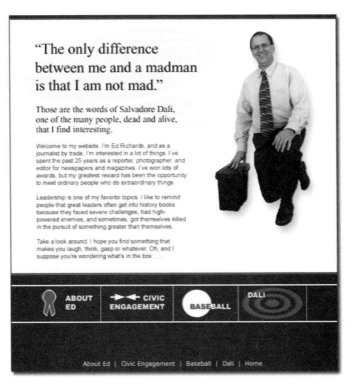

Figure 6.3 Personal Web Page in a Magazinelike Format

Designing Navigation

Navigation may be the single most important part of a Web site. If the viewer cannot get around easily and quickly, they will most likely move on to another Web site. Ideally, your navigation menu should contain no more than seven links. Try to group your content into as few categories as possible. Remember that depth is a unique feature of the Web. Look again at the flowchart in Figure 6.1. The largest volume of pages is deep into the site. A good Web site is like a pyramid or a large company's organization chart. The site begins with a single home page, then branches to a few categories, which then branch to multiple pages.

Navigation menus—or bars—may be placed at the top or bottom of the page or on the left side. Occasionally, you will see a right-side menu bar, but top and left-side bars are the most common. Whatever you choose, be sure to give the viewer a link or button to get back to the home page from every inside page on your site.

Figure 6.4 shows the home page and one of the inside pages. On the home page, this author wanted the viewer to read the text before presenting him or her with the menu, so the menu bar is at the bottom. However, once the viewer goes to an inside page, the navigation menu is always at the top where it will be easy to access from any page.

This type of juxtaposition also helps you define a different look for your home page. If every page looks just like the home page, the viewer may not realize where he or she is within the site. Be sure to do something on your home page to differentiate it from the inside pages. But remember that changing the design too much can be confusing.

In all your inside pages, be sure to remain consistent with your color scheme and the location of the navigation bar.

Figure 6.4 (a) Splash Screen Home Page; (b) One of the Inside Pages

Designing Above the Fold

Also in Figure 6.4, notice that the home page looks different than it does in Figure 6.3. It has been shortened so that the navigation menu now appears *above the fold.* "Above the fold" is a newspaper term that refers to placement of content above or below the horizontal fold in the newspaper. If something is above the fold, it is more likely to be seen and read.

For computer monitors set at 800 by 600 pixels, the fold in a Web page browser window falls at about line 420. If you do not want your users to have to scroll down, place your content above that line. You can use the Guide tool to denote the fold line while you are designing in Photoshop/ImageReady.

To shorten the home page that is shown in Figure 6.3, the author had to eliminate some of the text. Sometimes deletion is very hard for people to do. But remember that Web users are scanners—they look quickly at the contents of a page, and unless something grabs them, they move on.

It is better to make your site deep. That is, let the user keep clicking down into the content to read more. Notice that on the inside page at the right of Figure 6.4, various words in the text are links. If something captures the viewer's attention, the link can be clicked to read more. Also on the inside page at the right of Figure 6.4, notice that the page is taller. Usually, viewers do not mind scrolling down for inside-page content.

Sketching Design Layouts

For any given Web page, there are a number of possibilities for design. In fact, having a very simple design is one solution. For most Web pages, the content is the reason a viewer will first use the page. Once they are at the site, the design will help keep them there and will enhance their experience.

We add design elements to a Web page for two reasons:

☆ Efficient and effective design helps the viewer identify important information and navigate through the page or site.

☆ Design makes the viewer's experience more enjoyable.

Once you determine the content of your page, including the text, images, and navigation structure, draw in your sketchbook several rough design possibilities. Figure 6.5 shows nine possible layouts. In each, blue indicates placement for navigation, red indicates placement for images, and green indicates placement for text. The bottom three layouts show shortened pages that might be used for a home page splash screen. Most examples use multiple columns.

Sometimes it is best for novice designers to use fewer columns; working with and troubleshooting the Web page is easier. The number of images you have available will also play a big role in determining your design. Of course, there are many more possibilities than those shown in Figure 6.5. You can mix and match elements from several examples to get just the right design for your Web page.

When viewing Figure 6.5, keep in mind that the sketches use rectangles simply to identify placement of different types of content. Of course, your Web page design will not appear so boxlike because you will use transparent images, text with ragged right-hand margins, and other nonrectangular shapes.

◎◎ Backgrounds and Simple Rollovers

Use text, images, and buttons and/or bars for navigation, and begin to experiment with design. If you have access to the companion Web site, you can use elements and images to recreate the sample Web pages used in this chapter.

Figure 6.5 Thumbnail Sketches of Design Possibilities

Creating Background Graphics and Tiles

One of the great things about designing Web pages as opposed to print documents is the opportunity to use color and creative design without incurring extreme production costs. When designing a Web page, you can be creative not only with the content of the page but also with the background area of the page.

There are several methods for creating background images for Web pages:

☆ *Color:* The simplest background is white or another solid color. If you will be using a Web editor or hand-coding the HTML, you can specify the background color at that time. But you may wish to add the background color to your Photoshop page while you are designing, as it will affect the overall look and feel.

☆ *As Part of Other Images:* Figure 6.3 shows a large gray shape in the background of the page. It is a cartoon speech bubble that was created with the Custom Shapes tool. The shape adds interest and humor to the page, and it serves to draw the viewer's eye from the quote to the name Dali and then over to the picture. You could choose to save this shape along with the text on top of it as one or more individual images. When the images are displayed on the Web page, the bubble will be in the background of the text, just as it appears here. In the next chapter, you will learn how to cut out—or slice—the images for use on a Web page.

As a Full-Screen Background: The following is another method for using the shape shown in Figure 6.3 or any large image as a full-screen background. Turn off all layers except the ones containing the background image you wish to use, in this case the cartoon bubble. Use the Save for Web command to save this image as a GIF file that will be specified as the background image in your Web editor or in hand-coded HTML. More information about specifying the size of a full-screen background appears later in the chapter.

 Background Tiles: Using background tiles is another method for producing a background. Read on for more information about tiles.

Tiling

In the HTML code that makes up a Web page, there is a particular code for specifying a background image for a page. Because of the way HTML works, an image that is used as a background will repeat endlessly within the browser window. This is called **tiling**. If an image is very small, it will repeat many times within a normal-sized browser window. If you make the image large enough, it will not begin to repeat unless the browser window and the computer monitor are extremely large.

In the example shown in Figure 6.3, you might choose to save the cartoon bubble shape as a separate GIF file with a canvas size of 1300 pixels wide by 1100 pixels high. Refer to the information given earlier about the physical size of Web pages and the size of computer monitors to help you understand. By making a very large-sized image, you will be fairly sure that the background *will not tile* in most browser windows. Use the Image→Canvas Size menu to change the size of your document to make it large enough for a nontiling background image.

The Web page shown in Figure 6.3 also presents an opportunity for making a background image that *will* tile. Notice the dark colors across the top and bottom of the image, separated by the large white background. To create a background tile that includes all those elements, you can use the Single Column Marquee tool. This tool allows you to select a one-pixel-wide section of the complete image.

Using the Single Column and Single Row Marquee Tools

1. Click and hold in the Marquee Tools box in the top left corner of the Toolbox to reveal the fly-out menu.

2. Choose the Single Column Marquee tool.

3. Click in the top left corner of your image. You will see the selection. It is 1 pixel wide and extends for the length of your image.

4. While it is selected, choose Edit→Copy Merged from the menu at the top of the screen. When you use the Copy Merged command, you will copy everything visible in your image, not just the active layer.

5. Create a New document. Usually, Photoshop/ImageReady will automatically use the dimensions of anything you have recently copied for the size of the new document. (If not, use 1 pixel for the width, and specify a height based on the size of the image you copied.)

6. With the new document active, choose Edit→Paste. The image you copied will appear. Save your new document as a PSD file (so that you can edit it later if necessary), and then use Save for Web to save a GIF file for use in your Web site.

7. When you specify this 1-pixel-wide image as a background image on a Web page, the image will tile throughout the browser window, creating a seamless background.

8. You can also use this technique with a horizontal selection from an image by using the Single Row Marquee tool.

Using ImageReady to Preview a Background Tile in a Browser

Tiling is a function of the Internet browser, not Photoshop/ImageReady. To see the effect of tiling, you can use the GIF file as a background image on an actual Web page and view it in a browser.

Alternatively, you can use the special Preview function in ImageReady to see the tiled background without having to add it to an actual Web page first. (You can also use this technique to preview an animation, such as the one you completed in Chapter Five.)

1. If you have been working in Photoshop, switch to ImageReady by clicking the button at the bottom of the Toolbox. (The Preview technique does not work in Photoshop.)

2. From the File Menu, choose Output Settings→Background. In the box that appears, click to choose View Document As Background. Click OK.

3. From the File menu, choose Preview In. If the name of a Web browser, like Explorer, does not appear in the fly-out menu, choose Other and navigate to the browser application icon in your computer. Click Open.

4. The browser will open, and your image will be tiled throughout the window. There will also be a box of text with details about your image.

Interesting backgrounds can add a whole new dimension to your Web page. Experiment with the single column and single row marquee methods. In addition, you can use any-size image as a background tile. See Figure 6.6 for some examples of tiled backgrounds. You can even use a photograph as a background. Usually, you will save a photo as a JPG rather than a GIF file.

☆ WARNING Be Careful with Web Page Backgrounds

Be sure that the background is not so busy that it makes the text on your Web page difficult to read. Be sure there is plenty of contrast between the color of your text and the color of the background. If you use a large photograph as a background, you may want to apply the **Blur filter** to it first. Blurring the background is always a good way to make your text stand out. If you use a background image like the ones in the top center and in the bottom row of Figure 6.6, you may want to create a white or light-colored rectangle to place underneath your block of text to increase readability.

Figure 6.6 Examples of Tiled Background Images as They Appear on the Web

Once you've created a background image, you can use Photoshop's Save for Web command to save it for use with a Web editor or with hand-coded HTML.

For more advanced background creation techniques, see Chapter Eight for an explanation of Photoshop's Pattern Maker and ImageReady's Tile Maker filters.

Setting Up a Simple Rollover Behavior in Photoshop

It is common on the Web to see buttons that change their appearance when the mouse moves on top of them or when the button is clicked. This is called Rollover behavior. This type of interactivity adds interest to your Web page. Users like to "make things happen" on a Web page.

For this activity, use Photoshop to set up a Rollover behavior. Use the techniques you learned in Chapters Three and Four to create shapes for navigation buttons for your Web page. Use color, text, and shapes. Add effects such as drop shadows and beveled edges.

Look again at Figure 6.3. The navigation bar on that Web page was created entirely in Photoshop. The Text tool was used for the text. The Custom Shapes tool was used to create the icons for each of the buttons. The Line tool was used for the separators between buttons.

As shown in Figure 6.3, the navigation buttons are in their Normal position. That is the way they appear when the viewer first sees them.

For a Rollover behavior to occur, you must first create a Rollover State. A Rollover State is essentially another version of the same button. The color of the

text may change, a drop shadow or bevel may change, an object might appear or disappear—the possibilities are endless. In complex Rollover behaviors, when the user moves the mouse to one area of the screen, something may change in a totally different area of the screen. Surf the Web for examples of interesting Rollover behaviors.

As you see in Figure 6.7, two separate layers were created for the icon in the button. One icon is blue and one is red. When the blue layer is showing (click to reveal the eye icon in the far left column), the button will be in its Normal position. When the red layer is showing, the button will be in its Rollover State.

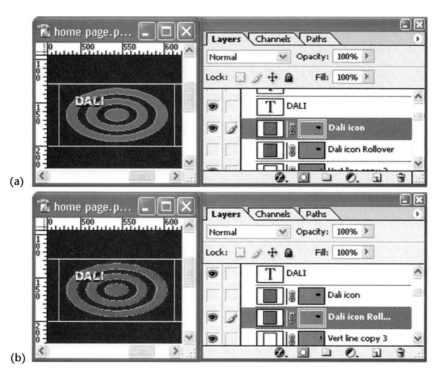

(a)

(b)

Figure 6.7 (a) Layer Setup for the Normal Position of a Button (b)Layer Setup for the Rollover State of the Same Button

To create a simple Rollover version of the normal button, follow these steps. Note that Showing and Hiding layers is the key technique for setting up a Rollover behavior.

☆ Create a duplicate layer of the button that will be used for the Normal position. With the button layer selected, choose Duplicate Layer from the Layer menu at the top of the screen or from the triangle menu at the top right of the Layers palette.

☆ To change the color of a shape, double-click inside the color rectangle in the shape's layer, and choose a new color from the color box that appears. To change the color of text, double-click inside the text box on the layer, and then choose a new color from the Options bar.

☆ In some cases, you do not need to create a duplicate layer to set up a simple Rollover behavior. For example, you might decide that in the Rollover State, a Glow or Bevel effect will be added to the button. You would then use the Show/Hide icons for the Effects on that layer to set up your Rollover behavior.

Once you've created multiple versions of a button, you can use Photoshop's Save for Web command to save images to be used with a Web editor or with hand-coded HTML. Show or Hide appropriate layers, and then save the image. Change the Show/Hide settings and save another image. You will program the actual Rollover behavior in your Web editor or with hand-coded HTML.

Alternatively, as you will learn in the next chapter, you can use ImageReady to do the Rollover programming for you.

◎◎ Saving a Showpeg

If you've followed along in this book so far, you've learned techniques for creating and saving individual images. You've also begun to design and create an entire Web page.

You may be ready to show your design to friends and family to solicit their comments. At this point, many designers use Photoshop's Save for Web command to create a JPG image of the entire page for use in gathering feedback.

Sometimes, designers call this image a "**showpeg**" (a word play on the term JPEG). You can print or e-mail this image, or you can open it in an Internet browser. It is a large picture of your entire Web page design, useful when you are first working out your design. A showpeg should never be used for your actual Web page.

Listening to others' comments, answering their questions, and taking some of their advice can help you design the best Web page possible.

Saving a Showpeg

☆ Summary

➤ Always begin with a plan. Many questions should be answered before you begin to design a Web page or site.

➤ You can use Photoshop to design your page and switch to ImageReady later to take advantage of its special Web features.

➤ Visually divide your page into rows and columns when you are creating a Web design.

➤ Navigation may be the single most important part of a Web site.

➤ Background colors and patterns can add interest to your Web page, but be sure to leave plenty of white space around text to make it readable.

➤ Menu buttons with Rollover behaviors add interest to your Web page.

➤ Save a showpeg of your design, and ask your friends and family for their feedback. Consider how you might make changes based on their comments.

☆ Online References

Communication Arts Annual Interactive Awards
`http://www.commarts.com/CA/interactive/`

Learn to Design with Web Developer
`http://www.webdeveloper.com/design/`

Mac Design Online Photoshop Tutorials
`http://www.macdesignonline.com/photoshop.html`

Web Style Guide
`http://www.webstyleguide.com/index.html?/`

Jakob Nielsen's Technology and Usability Site
`http://www.useit.com/`

WebMonkey Information Architecture Tutorial
`http://hotwired.lycos.com/webmonkey/design/site_building/`
`tutorials/tutorial1.html`

Web Sites that Suck
`http://www.websitesthatsuck.com/`

☆ Review Questions

1. What are the basic components of a Web page?

2. What is a typical physical size for Web pages today?

3. Why do you design a Web page with tables in mind?

4. What is the purpose of white space?

5. What is the most common location of the navigation bar on a Web page?

6. What is the reason for using a splash screen page?

☆ Hands-On Exercises

If you have access to the companion Web site for this book, use those files for the exercises.

1. Decide on a topic for a Web page. Write down the answers to the basic Web design questions listed at the beginning of this chapter.

2. Create a Color Guide for the Web page.

3. Create three different rough Web page designs, placing the navigation bar in different locations.

4. Set up the layers necessary to produce navigation buttons with Rollover behaviors. Use different colors, shapes, and effects.

5. Save a *showpeg* of your Web page, and ask for feedback from your family and friends. Consider the changes you might make based on their feedback.

CHAPTER SEVEN

PUBLISHING YOUR WEB PAGE

At this point, many readers of this book will want to take what they have learned so far and produce images that can be used with hand-coded HTML or with a Web editing program like Adobe Go Live, Macromedia Dreamweaver, or Microsoft Front Page. If so, the software and the techniques in this and previous chapters are invaluable. But Photoshop and ImageReady contain even more tools to assist you. In this chapter, you will learn special techniques for advanced processing of your Web images. You will also learn how to use Photoshop/ImageReady to create a complete Web page without needing to use a Web editor or do any HTML coding.

Chapter Objectives

☆ Use slices to optimize your Web images

☆ Use guides to create slices

☆ Set Slice Options

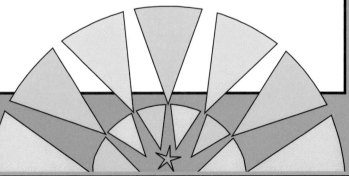

☆ Use live text in an ImageReady Web page

☆ Program Rollover buttons and Image Maps

☆ Optimize your images and set Output options

☆ Save your ImageReady document as a complete Web page

◎◎ Slicing a Web Page

You've no doubt visited a Web site where you waited a painfully long time for a large image to download onto the page. Although more and more people are using high-speed connections to the Internet, image size and download time are still factors in any Web page design. Photoshop and ImageReady include tools that allow you to **slice** an image into smaller sections, thus speeding up those long download times.

> ☆ TIP　**Using Slices with a Web Editor or Hand-Coded HTML**
>
> If you are using your ImageReady images with a Web editor or with a hand-coded HTML page, you might slice one large image into four sections. You would then arrange the sections in an HTML table with rows and columns. If there is no padding or spacing in the cells of the table, the image would appear precisely joined together, as though it were one large image. The viewer would probably not notice that the image had been sliced, but the download time would be much faster.

Learning to Use Slices

A slice is a rectangular area. It can be as large as the entire image, or it can be one of many slices in the same image.

To learn how to use slices, open ImageReady and create a new blank document. ImageReady includes more slicing tools than Photoshop, so you will use ImageReady throughout this chapter. Review Chapter Five to refresh your memory of the ImageReady work area.

Figure 7.1 shows the ImageReady CS Toolbox. The second tool down on the left is the Slice tool. Next to it, on the right, is the Slice Select tool.

In the ImageReady 7 Toolbox, look for the third tool down on the right. This is the Slice tool set. Click and hold the tool to reveal a fly-out menu that includes Slice tool and Slice Select tool. The Slice tools allow you to create and edit slices.

In the View menu at the top of the screen, choose View→Show to reveal a fly-out list of items. When there is a checkmark beside an item, it is active. In this chapter, we will use the View→Show→Guides and View→Show→Slices menu items. Notice also the Slices menu at the top of the screen. We will use that menu in this chapter as well.

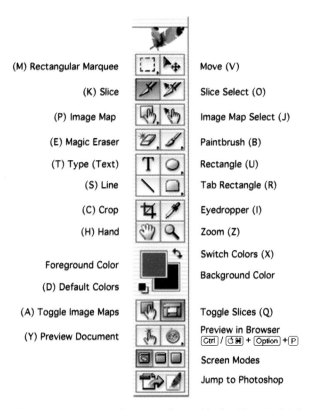

Figure 7.1 ImageReady CS Toolbox with the Slice Tool Selected

Creating Guides

Choose View→Rulers to make sure that the rulers are turned on. Using the Move tool, click inside one of the rulers and drag out onto the canvas to create a **guide**. Use the View→Show→Guides menu to turn the guides on and off.

Viewing Slices

Choose the View→Show→Slices menu item. You will see that your image is outlined and that a box with a number inside appears in the top left corner. Every new Photoshop or ImageReady document automatically contains one slice that encompasses the image. The first Slice is number one.

Creating Slices

1. Figure 7.2 shows what happens when you create a new slice. Choose the Slice tool from the Toolbox. Click, hold, and drag the Slice tool anywhere on the image to create another slice. When you do so, ImageReady automatically creates additional slices, if necessary, to keep all the slices in a row and column (table) format.

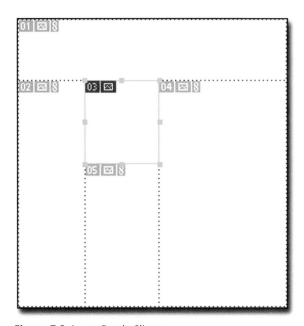

Figure 7.2 ImageReady Slices

2. Create several slices and watch how ImageReady generates additional slices. Each new slice has a unique number.

3. Now choose the Slice Select tool from the Toolbox. Click on one of the slices you created. It will become outlined in a different color to indicate that it is the selected slice.

☆ **TIP**   **Selecting More than One Slice at a Time**

To select more than one slice at a time, hold down the [Shift] key while you click on the slices.

User Slices

Notice that the slices you created have number boxes that are blue. The slices that ImageReady automatically generated have gray boxes. When the box is blue, it means that this is a User Slice. When you select a User Slice, it has small boxes—or handles—at the corners and middle of the selection outline. These boxes allow you to edit the size of the slice by dragging the boxes with the Slice Select tool. Try editing one of your slices now. Notice how the other slices change in accordance with your edits.

Auto Slices

The slices that ImageReady automatically creates—the ones with the gray number boxes—are called Auto Slices. Notice that when you select an Auto Slice, an outline appears around it, but you cannot edit the slice. To edit a slice, it must be a User Slice. You can change an Auto Slice into a User Slice by using the Slices menu at the top of the screen. Click on an Auto Slice you wish to change into a User Slice. From the Slices menu, choose Promote to User Slice. The number box will change to blue and the Slice will now be editable.

Deleting Slices

If you wish to delete any one or all of your slices, use the Slices menu. To delete a particular slice, click on it and choose Delete Slice from the Slices menu. To delete all the slices (except the original slice, which is always present), choose Delete All from the Slices menu.

Selecting All Slices and Deselecting Slices

The items in the Select menu at the top of the screen change depending on whether or not the Slice tool in the Toolbox is selected. To demonstrate what happens, choose the Move tool or another tool in the Toolbox. Click the Select menu and notice the items in the menu. Now choose the Slice tool in the Toolbox and notice the items in the Select menu. With the Slice tool chosen, you can use the Select menu to Select All Slices or Deselect Slices.

Slices from Guides

Now it's time to slice your design.

Open the Web page you designed in Chapter Six. If you don't have one, stop and create a quick design using text, shapes, colors, and an image. Lay out these elements using ideas from the sketches in Figure 6.5.

You can use guides to help you get started with your slices. First you create guides that mark the areas to be sliced. Then you use an ImageReady menu command to create slices based on your placement of the guides.

Creating Slices from Guides

On your design, create guides that denote the areas to be sliced. In Figure 7.3, notice the vertical guides that divide the navigation bar into smaller sections, one for each button. Notice the horizontal guides above and below the headline of the page. All these guides are marking areas where we want to slice the large image into smaller images.

1. When your guides are in place, choose Create Slices from Guides in the Slices menu at the top of the screen. All these slices have blue number boxes, meaning that they are User Slices.

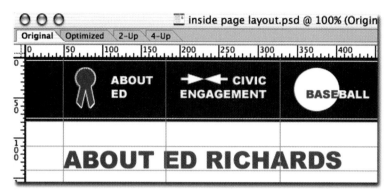

Figure 7.3 Guides Mark Areas Where Slices Will Be Created

2. Notice that the slices (and the guides) are laid out in rows and columns, as in a table. If you were thinking about tables when you designed your Web page, your page should lend itself well to the slicing procedure in ImageReady.

Editing Slices Created from Guides

Images download one at a time in an Internet browser. With slow connection speeds, some images appear before others. For this reason, slicing images into coherent pieces is a good idea.

In Figure 7.4(a), notice that the original guides and slices chop up the headline ("About Ed Richards") into three images. In Figure 7.4(b), the slices have been edited so that the complete headline is one slice. Now, when the headline image downloads into the browser window, it will appear as one coherent piece rather than several oddly divided pieces.

☆ **WARNING** Turn Guides Off After Slicing

You may wish to use the View menu to turn the guides off after you have created your slices. Otherwise, it may become difficult to see exactly where the slices are.

The following steps show how to edit slices created from guides.

1. Choose the Slice Select tool from the Toolbox. Click on one of the slices you wish to edit.

2. Click and drag on one of the handles on the slice and resize it.

3. Sometimes when you edit a slice, some of the original slices remain inside the dimensions of the slice you edited. If this happens, use the Slice Select tool to select those slices. In the Slices menu, choose Delete Slice.

4. Notice that in Figure 7.4(b), the areas for the headline and for the text have each been made into one slice.

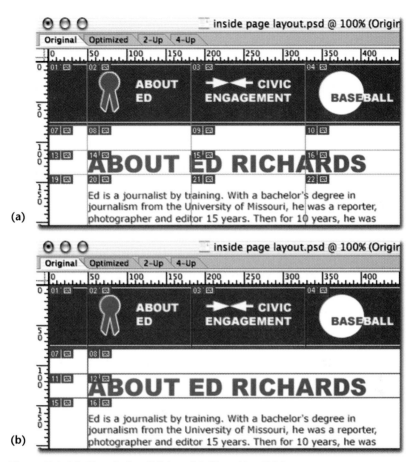

Figure 7.4 (a) Slices Before Editing, (b) Slices After Editing

Setting Slice Options

If you are going to use hand-coded HTML or a Web editing program like Adobe Go Live, Macromedia Dreamweaver, or Microsoft Front Page, you do not need to use ImageReady's slice options. You can set these options later. At this point, you would save your specific slices. Read the information about saving slices at the end of this chapter.

HTML is the computer programming code that tells an Internet browser how to display a Web page. If you do not know how to write HTML code or if you are not going to use a Web editing program, you can have ImageReady write the code for you. You can then save your document as a complete and functional Web page.

In this book, we are using the phrase "complete Web page" to indicate a design that has been saved along with the HTML file that is necessary to display the page in an Internet browser window.

To take advantage of this feature, you should assign certain Slice Options to each of your Slices. When you use these options, ImageReady creates *behind-the-scenes* HTML code that a browser will use to display the Web page.

☆ TIP   **Both Photoshop and ImageReady Create HTML Code**

In this chapter, you should work with ImageReady to take advantage of special features of the program. Photoshop also writes behind-the-scenes HTML code and can be used to save a complete Web page.

You set Slice Options for slices one at a time. If you set a Slice Option for an Auto Slice, the slice will become a User Slice.

1. Use the Window menu to open the Slice palette. Choose the Slice Select tool and click to select one of your slices.

2. Notice that various option boxes have become available in the Slice palette.

3. Use the dropdown menus to make choices, and enter appropriate information into the boxes. Read on for an explanation for each of these items.

4. Choose File→Preview In to open a browser where you can see the Web page, and test the links and other information you entered.

Refer to Figure 7.5 as you learn to use the following Slice Options. If you are using a version prior to ImageReady CS, the palette will look slightly different, but the same Slice Options will be available.

Type

The Type dropdown menu refers to the type of content the slice contains. The default setting is Image. Use this setting for the images and buttons on your page. Use No Image for areas that will contain either a solid background color or live text. See the sections "BG or Background" and "Live Web Text" for more information.

Name of Slice

The Name field is automatically filled in by ImageReady. The program uses special naming techniques based on the name you gave to the file and unique slice numbers for each slice in a document. Leave this area as is.

☆ WARNING   **File-Naming Techniques**

As a novice, you should not make changes to the automatic file-naming techniques used for Slices by ImageReady. As you become more advanced, if you wish to alter the naming technique ImageReady uses, you can use the **Output Settings→Saving Files** box to set up your own naming technique.

URL

The URL field is used for specifying a Web address that viewers will be taken to if they click on a button or other linked image. Type a complete Web address here, including http:// . (Advanced users can use Relative Links here.)

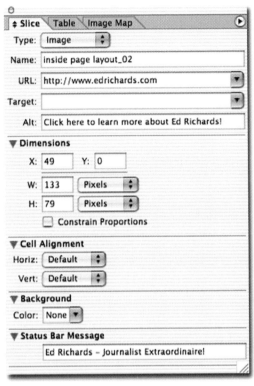

Figure 7.5 ImageReadyCS Slice Palette, Showing Slice Options for a Selected Slice

Target

The Target field is used for Web pages constructed with an advanced technique called Frames. Novice users should leave this field blank.

Alt Text

The Alt field allows you to enter text that explains the content of an image on a Web page. Alt text is used by viewers who are visually impaired or who need special equipment to view a Web page. Including Alt text for every image on your Web page ensures that everyone can understand and enjoy the content of your page. Alt text will also be displayed to all viewers while an image is downloading. In some browsers, Alt text will also pop up when the mouse is placed over the image.

Dimensions

The Dimensions field is used to alter the width and height of a slice. Novice users should leave this area as is.

Cell Alignment

Cell alignment is discussed in the following section, "Live Web Text."

BG or Background

The BG or Background dropdown menu refers to the background color of the slice. The default setting is None. When you click on the downward-pointing triangle to the right of the BG box, you can use a color palette to choose a background color.

You may have already created a colored or white Background layer in making a showpeg for getting feedback on your design (see Chapter Six). But when you are using ImageReady to create a complete Web page, it is probably better to Hide that Background layer and use the BG or Background setting in the Slice palette or the Optimize settings to add the background color. Later in this chapter, you will learn more about saving backgrounds.

Status Bar Message

The Message field allows you to enter content that will appear in the Status field at the bottom of a browser window when the viewer places their mouse over a button or other link on a Web page. If you do not enter a message, the URL for the link will be displayed in the Status field of the browser window.

Live Web Text

Your Web page will probably not be made up entirely of images. Whenever possible, you should use **live text** (see Chapter Four) to keep the size of your page small and the download time short. On the Web page shown in Figure 7.6, slice 16 is the area where live text will be placed.

You may have created a text layer in order to make a showpeg and get feedback on your design (see Chapter Six). But when you are using ImageReady to create a complete Web page, you should Hide that text layer. Use the Slice palette and the No Image option to add the text. When you select No Image, a box for text appears.

After you type or copy text into the Text box (as shown in Figure 7.6) in the Slice palette, use the File➔Preview In menu to view the page in a browser. The text will not appear on your ImageReady document.

Cell Alignment

In the Slice palette, when you choose the No Image setting, Cell Alignment pop-up menus allow you to set the alignment options for the text. Use Horiz to set the horizontal alignment for the text—left, right, or center.

You can also set the vertical alignment of the block of text as it appears in the table. By default, in a browser, live text is always centered within the height of the cell it appears in. Sometimes you want to be sure that the text always aligns with the top or bottom of the cell. Use the Vert pop-up menu in the Cell Alignment area of the Slice palette to set this option.

☆ **TIP   Table Cells**

Tables are created with rows and columns. The areas created by the intersection of rows and columns are called *cells*.

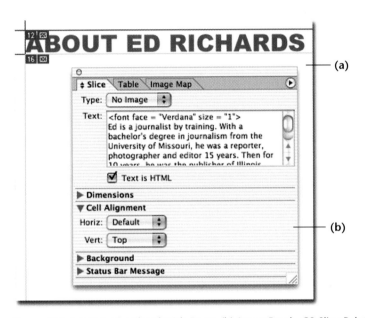

Figure 7.6 (a) Part of a Sliced Web Page; (b) ImageReady CS Slice Palette Showing the No Image, Text Is HTML, and Cell Alignment Options

HTML 101

When you enter text into the No Image text box on the Slice palette, it will appear in a browser with the default text settings specified by the browser. Default browser settings most often use a serif font, usually Times New Roman.

In Chapter Four, you learned that on a Web page, large bodies of small text often look more attractive and are more readable when a sans serif font is used. By learning to write a small bit of HTML coding, you can alter the display of live text in an ImageReady Web page.

Notice in Figure 7.6 that the box Text is HTML is checked. When you check this box, you can add HTML code to the body of text so that it will display with a specific font in a specific size. HTML code uses formatting tags, surrounded by angle brackets, at the beginning and end of the content, to instruct the browser how to display the content of the Web page.

Figure 7.6 includes the following code at the beginning of the text:

```
<font face = "Verdana" size = "1">
```

In this code, the font specified is Verdana and the size of the font is 1. You are probably used to using font sizes of 12, 14, 24, and so on. But in basic HTML, font sizes are expressed with the numbers 1 through 7, –1 through –7, and +1 through +7. You can experiment with various sizes to see their effects on the size of the text.

HTML code must be very exact, so use the code just as it is shown, substituting a different font name and size if you wish. Remember that Times New Roman, Verdana, and Arial are fonts that almost every computer contains. If you specify a particular font that the user's computer does not contain, the browser will use its default font.

When you use a font-formatting tag at the beginning of your text block in the Slice palette, you must also use a closing tag at the end of the block of text.

To close the font tag shown, add this to the end of your text block:

```
</font>
```

When you use a forward slash (/) in a tag, it tells the browser to end the instructions that were begun by the tag at the beginning of the content. In this case, you are telling the browser that you are finished using the font tag.

There are two more simple HTML tags you may wish to use with live text in an ImageReady Web page. The following tags deal with the spacing between lines of text.

HTML code ignores the normal Returns (Enters) you use in order to skip a line when you are typing. You must use a paragraph tag when you want to skip a line or a *break tag* when you want to go to the next line without skipping a line.

```
<p> and </p>
```

These are paragraph tags. When placed at the beginning and end of a block of text, they instruct the browser to leave an entire line of space at the beginning of a text block.

```
<br>
```

This is the break tag. It does not need a closing tag. When placed at the end of a line of text, it instructs the browser to start on the next line with any following text without skipping a line.

Almost anyone can learn to write HTML code. It is fun and pretty easy. At the end of this chapter, you will find some URLs for Web sites that teach HTML coding.

◎◎ Using the Optimize Settings

You can apply Optimize settings to slices so that different sections of the document can be uniquely processed for the Web. In Chapters One, Two, and Three, you learned that graphic images are best processed in the GIF format. Photographs are best processed in the JPG format.

Once you have sliced your ImageReady document, click on each slice and use the Optimize palette to select optimizing options for each slice. You learned to use ImageReady's Optimize palette in Chapter Five. You also learned about optimizing your images with Photoshop's Save for Web command in Chapters One, Two, and Three. Use the information from all these chapters as you decide how to apply Optimize settings to your slices.

◎◎ Creating Rollover Behavior

If you are going to use hand-coded HTML or a Web editing program like Adobe Go Live, Macromedia Dreamweaver, or Microsoft Front Page, you do not need to use ImageReady to program a Rollover behavior. You can program the behavior later. At this point, you would save the specific slices that are associated with the Rollover behavior. Read information about saving slices at the end of this chapter.

Rollover images are commonly used on the Web. When the mouse is placed over a Rollover button or image, an alternate version of the button or image appears.

Programming a Rollover Behavior

In Chapter Six, you set up a simple Rollover behavior with Photoshop by creating an alternate version of a particular button. Now you can use ImageReady to create a complete Web page, using the Rollover palette in ImageReady 7 or the Web Content palette in ImageReady CS to program the Rollover behavior. (You cannot program Rollovers in Photoshop.)

1. Be sure you have created the alternate version of your button or link by creating a duplicate layer or adding effects. (Review the information in Chapter Six.)

2. Use the Window menu to open the Rollovers palette or the Web Content palette. Notice that every slice in your document is shown as a separate layer. Find and select the slice for the button you wish to program with a Rollover behavior (Figure 7.7(a)).

3. In Photoshop 7, from the triangle menu at the top right of the Rollovers palette, choose New Rollover State. A new layer will appear in the palette under the layer for the button you wish to program. If it is not automatically selected, select this new layer. In the Rollover palette, from the triangle menu, choose Rollover State Options. Notice that several options are available. The most commonly used option is Over. Click to select Over, and click OK.

4. In Photoshop CS, select the Web Content palette. Use the triangle menu at the top right of the Web Content palette to choose New Rollover State. The new layer will automatically be named Over (Figure 7.7(c)). If you wish to change the type of state, choose Rollover State Options from the triangle menu.

5. Be sure your Over layer is selected. In your regular Layers palette, Hide and Show layers or effects to reveal the alternate version of your button (Figure 7.7(b)).

6. You might also create additional alternate versions of a button for other Rollover states. For example, different images could appear when the mouse is held down or clicked, when the mouse is let up, or when the mouse moves out of the button area. By default, if you do not program any other Rollover behaviors, the button will return to its normal state when the mouse moves up, down, out, or is clicked.

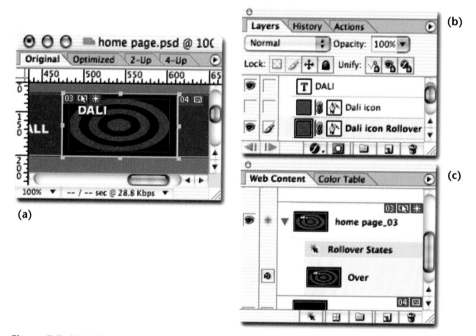

Figure 7.7 (a) Web Page Button, (b) the Layers Palette, (c) the Photoshop CS Web Content Palette Showing the "Over" Rollover State

Using Prebuilt Rollover Styles

In Chapters Three and Four, you learned to use Photoshop's Styles palette to add prebuilt styles to a button or graphic. ImageReady also contains a Styles palette, and it includes some custom prebuilt Rollover styles you can use when you save a complete Web page in ImageReady.

You might also save and use the individual images from the automatically created Rollover states for a page created in a Web editor or with hand-coded HTML.

In the Styles palette, several of the style boxes contain a black triangle in the top left corner. If you create a shape and add one of these styles to it, it will automatically program prebuilt Rollover behaviors with one or more alternate states.

Create a new document, draw a shape, and experiment with these styles. Once you apply a prebuilt Rollover style, you can click on any of the automatically created elements of the style in the regular Layers palette and change colors, effects, and so on.

◎◎ Using Simple Image Maps

If you are going to use hand-coded HTML or a Web editing program like Adobe Go Live, Macromedia Dreamweaver, or Microsoft Front Page, you do not need to use ImageReady to create an **image map**. You can set up the image map with HTML or with your Web editor.

Image maps allow you to make any portion of an image a link to a URL.

Unlike rectangular images or slices, an image map can be almost any shape. Thus, you can designate an irregularly shaped image or portion of an image to be a clickable link.

On a Web page about automobile racing, you might use an image map to make the exact shape of a car clickable. On a Web page about wildflowers, with a large image containing several different flowers, you could use image maps to make each separate flower a link to its own Web page.

Image maps are best used when the rectangular shape of slices does not provide exactly the shape you need for a link.

You create an image map by using the Image Map tool. This tool allows you to outline the part of an image that you want to be a link to another Web page.

Figure 7.8 shows the Image Map tools in the Toolbox, an image that has been mapped with the Polygon image map tool, and the Image Map palette.

To create an image map, follow this procedure:

1. Find an image on your Web page that you would like to *map* to a URL. In the example shown in Figure 7.8, instead of making the entire rectangular Slice a link to a URL, an Image Map was used to outline only the picture of a person.

2. Choose one of the Image Map tools in the Toolbox (Figure 7.8(a)). You can use the Rectangle, Circle, or Polygon tool. The Polygon image map tool allows you to carefully outline an irregularly shaped object.

3. To use the Polygon tool, click to establish a point, move the mouse and click again to establish another point, repeat this process without stopping until you encircle the entire object, and then double-click on the first point to end the map. It may take some practice to get this right (Figure 7.8(b)).

4. To remove an image map, use the Image Map Select tool, click on the image map, and use the [Delete] key on your keyboard.

5. When you have created an image map, use the Image Map palette (Figure 7.8(c)) to specify a URL link and add Alt text. The Image Map palette options are similar to the Slice palette options explained earlier in this chapter.

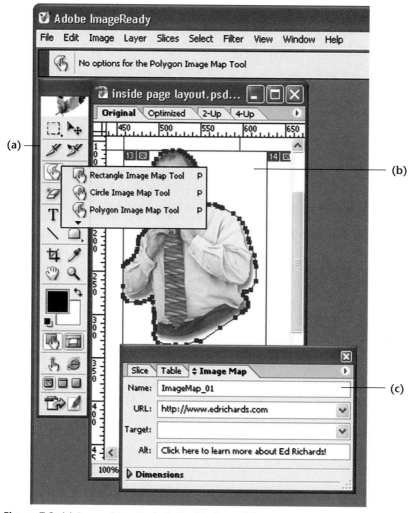

Figure 7.8 (a) Image Map Tools in the Toolbox, (b) an Image with an Image Map, (c) the Image Map Palette

There are several advanced techniques available for image maps, but this book deals only with simple image maps, such as the one shown here.

◎◎ Setting the Output Options

Once you have sliced your Web design, chosen options for the slices, programmed rollovers, and created image maps, you are ready to save the design as a Web page or as a series of images you will use with a Web editor or hand-coded HTML.

Before you save, you should decide on the various **output options**. Novices should leave most of these options at their default settings.

☆ From the File menu, choose Output Settings→HTML. Novices should not change the default settings, but notice the items included in this box so that you will begin to become familiar with the *jargon* of HTML. If, for some reason, Custom Settings is showing in the Settings area at the top of the box, change it in the pop-up menu to Default Settings.

☆ There are two ways to move to the next box of settings. Choose a setting from the pop-up box at the top left, or, on the right side of the box, choose Next. Use the same techniques to reveal any of the settings boxes.

☆ Photoshop/ImageReady CS includes a box called Saving HTML Files. If you are a novice, leave these settings at the default values.

☆ In the Slices and Image Maps boxes, novices should leave the settings at the default values.

☆ You already used the Background settings box in Chapter Six when you previewed the background image you created. Read on for a complete explanation of methods for saving backgrounds.

☆ The Saving Files box includes the File Naming technique that ImageReady will use to name the Slices in your document. Novices should not change the default settings of the File Naming section. The Filename Compatibility section allows users to make their file names compatible with Windows, Mac, and Unix computer systems. In the Optimized Files section, you can check Put Images in Folder and name the folder (usually you should name it "images"). See the information in the next section to learn how to copy background images when you are saving.

In Photoshop/ImageReady 7, you can add more information in the Saving Files box. A check beside Include Copyright allows you to include a Title for your Web page that will appear at the top of the browser window in the title bar. To utilize this feature, choose File Info from the File menu and enter a Title in the Caption field. You can also enter copyright information. The copyright information will not appear to the viewer but will be saved in the HTML code that makes up the Web page. In Photoshop/ImageReady CS, use the File Info box to enter copyright, title, and other information. It will automatically be saved with your Web page files.

Saving Background Colors or Images

There are three ways to deal with background colors or images when you save a Web page.

Background Is a Separate File

Remember that if you have a separate file that you *do not wish to tile* in the background (for example, the cartoon bubble in the background of the Web page design in Chapter Six), set the physical size, or Canvas Size, of the file to approximately 1100 pixels wide by 800 pixels high. This is called a Full Screen Background. If you *do wish to tile* the image, it can be as small as 1 pixel wide and/or high (for example, the single row and column selections used as examples in Chapter Six or a small tile that you create or download from a Web resources site). Please don't forget that busy backgrounds often make Web pages unreadable.

When you have a separate file you are using for a background, make sure you Hide (eye icon off) the Background layer of your Web page document. When you set the Optimize settings for each of the slices, you should use the GIF format and check Transparency On. Choose an appropriate Matte color if you want to eliminate the "halo" effect around images in the slices. This is especially important if you have images that are irregularly shaped and do not constitute a complete rectangle of color or image material.

In the Background section of the Output Settings box, choose View Document as Image. In the Background Image→Path section, navigate to identify the separate file that will be used as a background. In the Saving Files section of the Output box, if you check the box Copy Background Image when Saving, your separate Background file will be copied into your Web site folder. It is a good idea to also check Put Images in Folder and to name that folder "images". All your slices, along with the separate Background image you specified, will be saved to the folder.

Background Color or Image Is Part of the Slices in the Design

You can choose to Show the Background layer of your design (eye icon on) so that the color or image will be saved as part of the slices when you save your Web page. When you set the Optimize settings for each of the slices, you should check Transparency Off. In the Saving Files section of the Output box, do not check Copy Background Image when Saving. All your slices will include the Background color or image.

Background Color Is Specified When Saving, Not During Design

If you design a Web page without including a color or image as a Background layer, you can specify a particular color to be used as a background when the Web page is saved. When you set the Optimize settings for each Slice, you should check Transparency On. In the Background section of the Output Settings box, choose View Document as Image, and leave the Background Image Path blank. In the pop-up menu labeled BG Color, choose a background color for the page.

◎◎ Saving a Web Page

When your Output options are set, you are ready to save the document and/or specific images in the document. Don't forget to choose Save from the File menu to save your PSD file. Then use the following guidelines to save your Web page.

Saving the Document as a Complete Web Page

1. Choose the Slice Select tool in the Toolbox, and then choose Select→All Slices.

2. From the File menu, choose Save Optimized.

3. In the box that appears, navigate to the desktop of your computer, and choose or create a folder for your Web page and images.

4. Usually, the home page, or first page of a Web site is named *index.html* or *index.htm*. Doing so simplifies the name of the URL you will use when you refer people to your Web site. You will only need to tell them the name of the Web site, not the name of the site plus the name of the home page. This special feature is a function of the server where your Web site resides. (A *server* is a computer that is connected to the Internet and is capable of displaying Web pages.)

5. In the Format pop-up menu, choose HTML and Images. ImageReady will save all the behind-the-scenes HTML coding necessary to display your page in a browser, along with all your images, rollovers, and so on.

6. In the Settings pop-up menu, the word Custom will appear if you have changed any of the Output Options explained earlier. If you have not changed any of the options, Default Settings will appear. If you want to change any of the options now, choose Other. The Output Options box will appear and you can make changes.

7. In the Slices pop-up menu, choose All Slices to save all the slices you created in the document. If you want to save only specific slices, be sure that only those slices are selected in the document, and choose Selected Slices.

8. Click Save and everything you selected will be saved in the location you specified. Check with the administrator of the server where your Web site will reside for information about uploading your site to the server.

9. Now that you have one complete Web page, you can use it as a template for additional pages that will have the same general design.

Saving Specific Slices but Not Behind-the-Scenes HTML Coding

1. Choose the Slice Select tool, and hold down the Shift key to select the slices that you want to save. If you want to save all the slices, be sure the Slice Select tool is selected and choose Select→All Slices.

2. From the File menu, choose Save Optimized.

3. In the box that appears, navigate to the Images folder in your Web site folder.

4. In the Format pop-up menu, choose Images Only.

5. Use the Settings pop-up menu to change any of your Output settings if necessary.

6. In the Slices menu, choose All Slices or Selected Slices, and then click Save.

As you can see, ImageReady gives you plenty of flexibility for saving your document and processing your images for the Web. Saving a complete Web page with ImageReady is best used for simple Web pages. If something does not appear correctly on your Web page, it will be difficult for you to troubleshoot the problem unless you know how to read and write HTML code.

Saving a Web Page

At the end of this chapter, you will find some URLs for sites that teach you to how to write HTML code. It is not terribly difficult, and if you plan to become a Web designer, you should probably learn HTML coding.

Using ImageReady to save a complete Web page can be very valuable for a beginner. It will give you a taste of HTML, and it will give you a good foundation for understanding how to use a Web editor like Adobe Go Live, Macromedia Dreamweaver, or Microsoft Front Page. It can also be very valuable for those who wish to go on to learn to use the Web program called Flash.

Even if you use a Web editor or hand-code HTML, you can start with a page created from ImageReady. All the HTML code is accessible and editable by hand or by a Web editor.

☆ Summary

▷ Slicing large images into smaller sections can improve the download time of your Web page.

▷ After you design a Web page, you can set guides to mark the areas that will be sliced and then create slices from guides.

▷ You can edit slices so that they include exactly the content you wish.

▷ You can use ImageReady slices with a Web editor or with hand-coded HTML, or you can save a complete Web page that includes the HTML file.

▷ If you plan to save a complete Web page, you can use ImageReady to set up links, Rollovers, browser messages, Alt text, image maps, and areas for live text.

▷ When you save an ImageReady file, you can choose whether or not to save the HTML document. You can also choose to save some or all of the slices.

▷ Saving a complete Web page with ImageReady can be a valuable experience for a novice Web designer. It can also be useful for those who will use a Web editor or hand-coded HTML because ImageReady's HTML document is completely editable.

▷ Novice designers should eventually learn to write or understand basic HTML code.

☆ Online References

UIUC's NCSA Beginner's Guide to HTML
`http://archive.ncsa.uiuc.edu/General/Internet/WWW/HTMLPrimer.html`

HTML Goodies Basic HTML Primer
`http://www.htmlgoodies.com/primers/basics.html`

WebMonkey HTML Tutorial
`http://hotwired.lycos.com/webmonkey/teachingtool/index.html`

Sun Microsystems, Inc.—Designing for Accessibility
`http://www.sun.com/access/developers/software.guides.html`

Bobby—Check Your Site for Accessibility
`http://bobby.watchfire.com/bobby/html/en/index.jsp`

☆ Review Questions

1. Why is it a good idea to slice large Web page images?

2. What is the difference between a User Slice and an Auto Slice?

3. How do you go about creating slices from guides?

4. Name two types of Rollover States.

5. Why would you create an image map?

☆ Hands-On Exercises

If you have access to the companion Web site for this book, use those files for the exercises.

1. Create a rough Web page design and create guides to mark the areas that will be sliced.

2. Slice the page and edit the slices.

3. Create an area for live text.

4. Add simple HTML font tags and view the results in a browser.

5. Create a Rollover button with at least two states other than the Normal one.

6. Save the Web page with ImageReady, including the HTML file, and view the results in a browser.

CHAPTER EIGHT

BEYOND THE BASICS

Photoshop and ImageReady are powerful applications that will revolutionize the way you create Web pages. Instead of humble little headlines and badly scanned photos, your pages will shout LOOK AT ME! Your pages will appear so professionally produced, they will instantly garner credibility.

As you learn to master the techniques presented in this book so far, you will undoubtedly come across things you want to do but do not know how. The tools, tips, and techniques summarized in this chapter will help you take your skills to the next level. In most cases, these techniques assume that you have mastered the information and procedures presented in Chapters One through Seven. And if you master all the techniques presented in this chapter, there are plenty more out there.

◉◉ Chapter Objectives

☆ Use the Help menus in Photoshop and ImageReady when you forget something or want to learn a new technique

☆ Learn several new tools and techniques

☆ Proceed at your own pace, using the information presented here only when you feel ready to attempt something new

◎◎ Getting Help

It takes a lot of practice to master the features of Photoshop and ImageReady. Don't be afraid to experiment and try things on your own. Keep this book as a handy reference, using the table of contents, index, and charts at the back of the book when you need specific information. There are many other sources for help as well.

While you are learning, here are more resources for assistance:

☆ The Help menu located at the top right of the screen offers well-organized, easy-to-understand instructions for everything covered in this book and more.

☆ You can also use the URLs listed at the end of each chapter in this book to find new information and techniques.

☆ If you have access to the companion Web site for this book, you will find sample files, updated URLs, and other resources there.

☆ To share information, you may want to set up an informal group of Photoshop users among your friends and acquaintances.

In Photoshop CS and later versions, the Help menu contains a new feature called How To tips. These tips are organized into convenient categories such as How to Create Web Images, How to Fix and Enhance Photos, and How to Paint and Draw. You can even create your own How To tips and add them to the Help menu. Also available from the Help menu, the Welcome screen includes links to tutorials and expert tips.

◎◎ Tools, Tips, and Techniques

Following, in alphabetical order, is a list of tools, tips, and techniques that will further help you master Photoshop/ImageReady for the Web. Each item includes a brief summary and assumes that you will experiment on your own and seek Help when you need it.

Of course, there are many other techniques than the ones presented here. This collection, however, includes the items most commonly sought out by beginning designers.

Actions

Use the Window menu at the top of the screen to reveal the Actions palette. Included here are several prebuilt actions that automate particular techniques. Photoshop and ImageReady have different prebuilt actions (Figure 8.1). Click the triangle next to an action name to reveal layers that list the steps for the technique. At the bottom of the Actions palette are buttons that allow you to Play, Stop, and Record an action.

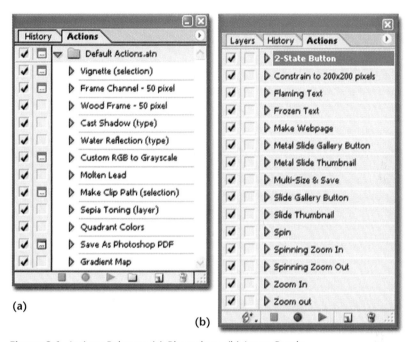

(a)

(b)

Figure 8.1 Actions Palettes: (a) Photoshop, (b) ImageReady

To use actions, open an image and click on the first layer of an action. Then click the Play button. Photoshop/ImageReady will then automatically apply the technique to your image. You can modify the steps in any of the prebuilt actions, and you can record your own actions. Some Web sites offer free actions that you can download and use to create new and interesting effects. Record your own actions when you find that you are applying the same techniques to a batch of images. It will make your work go faster.

Blending Modes

When you use the Painting tools in Photoshop and ImageReady, a pop-up menu at the top of the Layers palette contains a list of blending modes. These items offer you different ways to blend the color you are using into the existing color of the layer you are working on. In most cases, the resulting blend will look different than either the existing color or the color you use for painting. Experiment with different blending modes to see the effects they create. In Photoshop's Help menu, go to the Index and look under Blending Modes for a complete list of the modes and the effects they create.

Canvas Size

Be sure you understand the difference between **image size** and **canvas size**. For example, you may want a uniform canvas size for all the navigation buttons on a Web page. But the images in each of the canvases may be different sizes. Sometimes you will need to enlarge the canvas to make sure that certain effects are visible. For example, if you draw a 3-inch square on an 8½-by-11-inch sheet of paper, the sheet of paper is the canvas. The square is the image. If you have an image that completely covers the canvas, and you add a drop shadow to the image, you will have to enlarge the canvas size in order to see the shadow. To change the canvas size, choose Image➜Canvas Size from the menu at the top of the screen.

Color Replacement Tool

Photoshop CS and later versions include a Color Replacement tool. This tool makes it easy to replace any color in an image. For example, you may wish to replace the brownish grass with a brighter shade of green grass in an outdoor photo. Locate the Healing Brush, the fourth tool down on the left side of the Toolbox. Click and hold to reveal the fly-out menu of additional tools. Choose the Color Replacement tool. Choose a Foreground Color in the Toolbox. This will be the new color you are adding to the photo.

Choose a brush size in the Options bar. For Mode, choose Color. This will be your most common selection, but you can experiment with the other choices. For Sampling, choose Continuous to sample a range of colors as you drag across the area you wish to change. Choose Once to click on a specific area of color and thus replace only that color. Choose Background Swatch to change only areas containing the background color. For Limits, choose Discontiguous or Contiguous depending on whether or not you want to replace connected colors as you mouseover the image. Use Find Edges to maintain crisp edges on parts of your image while you are replacing colors. Use the Tolerance setting to select more or less pixels of similar color. Check Anti-Aliased to define a smooth edge while you are painting with the Color Replacement tool.

Now drag on the parts of the photo you wish to change. You will be replacing the old color with the new color you selected in the Toolbox.

You can also use the Color Replacement tool to correct red eyes in photographs. See "Red Eye Correction" in this chapter.

Contact Sheet

You may already—or will soon—have lots of pictures and images in your Master Originals folder. To help you keep track of what you have, use the **contact sheet** feature in Photoshop to create a preview page with small thumbnails of several images. In the File menu, choose Automate➜Contact Sheet II. In the box that appears, choose a Source Folder where your pictures reside. Identify the size of the document—or canvas—you wish to use. Then choose the layout options for the thumbnails, that is, how many pictures will appear in each row and column of the contact sheet. If you check Use Filename as Caption, each thumbnail will be identified by the existing name of the file. When you click OK, Photoshop will automatically browse the contents of your source folder and create thumbnails in the layout you specified. You can print this document and use it to review your picture collection. Or you can keep it inside the source folder, where it will be handy for later review when you are trying to locate a particular image. See Figure 8.2 for an example of a contact sheet.

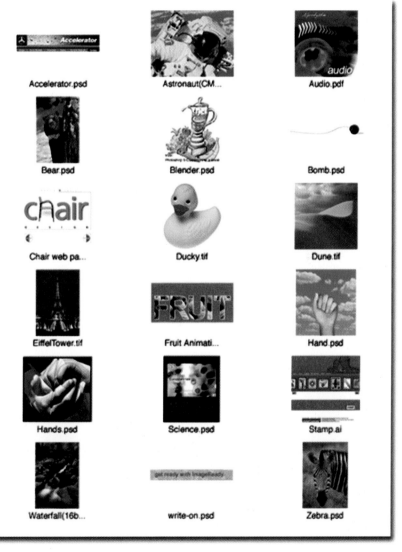

Figure 8.2 Contact Sheet Showing Thumbnails of Various Types of Images

Design

You can—and should—learn good design. It just takes practice, practice, practice. Designing for the Web presents different challenges than when designing for print. Don't forget to test your designs and get feedback. Then make changes to accommodate some of the idiosyncrasies of the Web. As the Web evolves, it will serve you well to know how to draw and how to make motion graphics. Practice drawing with the Vector tools. Create and test many animations. If you refine these skills, you will be ready to face the future of Web design.

Directory Structure

Stay organized. In no time at all you will have hundreds of files. Name them correctly, as explained in Chapter One. Use the saving strategy explained in Chapters One and Two. When you create a Web site, make a folder (directory) with the name of your Web site. Inside, put all the HTML files that make up the site. Also make a folder called "images" for all the GIF and JPG images that will appear on your Web pages. (Photoshop and ImageReady can do this for you, as explained in Chapter Seven.) If you put all your images with the HTML files, rather than inside an images folder, it may eventually become difficult to manage the files and troubleshoot your Web site. And don't forget to make a Project folder where you can keep all the related PSD images and other documents you use while creating the site.

Figure 8.3 shows a Master Originals folder (Figure 8.3(a)), a Project Files folder (Figure 8.3(b)), and a Web site folder (Figure 8.3(c)). Notice that the name of the Web site folder and the files it contains (Figure 8.3(d)) conform to the naming guidelines explained in Chapter One. This is important because these files and the folder will be used on the Internet. The HTML files are the individual Web pages. The *images* folder contains all the images for the site. The Project Files folder contains the originals of the images and some original text documents. These files will not appear on the Web site, but it is important to keep them so that you can go back to do further editing if needed. The Master Originals folder contains the designer's original, unedited images.

Disjointed (or Remote) Rollovers

In this book, you learned to make a button change its appearance when the mouse moves on top of it. Another interesting type of Rollover behavior is the **disjointed** (or **remote**) Rollover, where something in another location on the page changes when you mouseover a button. You can use this idea when you are creating a complete Web page in ImageReady or when you are using a Web editor or writing hand-coded HTML. ImageReady can program the Rollover for you, or you can do the programming with HTML.

Be sure to make all the necessary images first. If you are programming the Rollover in ImageReady, when you set up the Rollover State, Hide or Show a layer containing the *disjointed image* instead of just changing the original button. ImageReady will then automatically write the HTML code to include the disjointed Rollover effect. In the example shown in Figure 8.4, when the viewer rolls over each of the link buttons on the left, a different explanatory message appears in the box to the right.

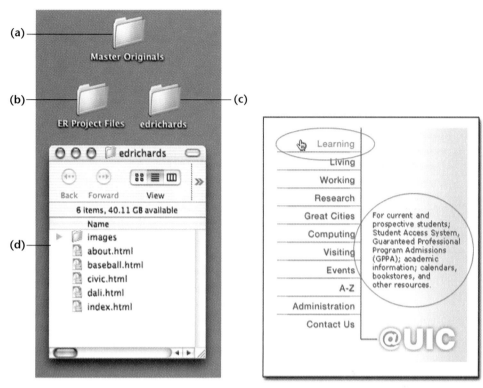

Figure 8.3 (a) Master Originals Folder, (b) Project Files Folder, and (c) Files and Folders in a (d) Web Directory

Figure 8.4 Example of a Disjointed Rollover.

Sometimes you create disjointed Rollovers by accident. If you do not want this accident to happen, be sure that you do not Hide or Show any layers that should not be affected by the Rollover while you are programming your Rollover States.

Docking Bar (Palette Well)

While you are creating and editing images with Photoshop and ImageReady, your work area quickly becomes crowded with palettes. Even if you have a large monitor, there are times when you can hardly see the image you are working on because you have so many palettes open. One handy solution is to store your most frequently used palettes in the Docking Bar, or Palette Well. For example, if you want to dock the Layers palette, open the Layers palette and drag the tab named Layers up to the area at the top of the work area on the far right. This area probably already contains a Brushes tab. As you drag and drop, the area will become highlighted, meaning you can let go of the mouse. The tab for the palette you dragged will now reside in the Docking Bar, or Palette Well, making it handy for future use. Click the tab to reveal the palette, and click the tab again to close the palette. This technique works only with monitors set at a resolution of at least 800 by 600; a resolution of 1024 by 768 or greater is recommended.

Drop Caps

Many books use the drop cap technique to draw the reader's eye to the first sentence in a chapter or section. A drop cap is the first letter (or first word) of a sentence made larger than the rest of the words and top aligning with the first line so that it drops down into the text. Sometimes it appears within a decorative box. You can use the drop cap technique on a Web page, too. Just don't overdo it—one per page is probably plenty. Use Photoshop/ImageReady to create an image for your drop cap. The placement will be easier to control than if you use live text in a Web editor or with hand-coded HTML. Figure 8.5 shows a news article that uses a drop cap on a *New York Times Online* Web page.

Figure 8.5 Drop Cap Used in an Article in the *New York Times Online*.
Copyright © 2003 by the New York Times Co. Reprinted with permission.

Drop Shadows and Other Layer Effects

Drop shadows—and other effects—add depth and dimension to the images, headlines, and subheads on your Web page. Experiment with the settings to create unusual and compelling shadows. Try different angles for the source of the shadow and other colors besides black or gray as the shadow color. But remember that too much of a good thing can be tacky. Be tasteful instead.

Duplicate Layer

When you get the urge to experiment, make a duplicate layer so that you do not destroy your original image. If you don't like the experiment, you can delete that layer and still have your original intact. Photoshop provides a particularly useful feature with the Duplicate Layer command. In the box that appears when you choose Duplicate Layer, you can assign a name for the new layer. You can also choose a specific Destination for the new layer. If you have another Photoshop image open at the same time, you can choose to send the new duplicate layer to that image. Or you can choose New to create a brand-new document. This is a useful technique when you want to take part of one document and include it in another document. ImageReady allows you to create duplicate layers only within the same document.

Export to Macromedia Flash (SWF)

ImageReady CS or later version: You can use ImageReady to export a complete document or individual layers as a Macromedia Flash (.swf) file. You can place the exported file on a Web page, or you can import it into Macromedia Flash. You will lose any Rollover behaviors or image maps in the process, but URL links added via the Slice options will be retained. To export a complete document, choose File→Export→Macromedia Flash SWF. In the box that appears, you can choose whether or not you wish to have an HTML file generated automatically. If you are not familiar with Flash, leave the other settings at their default values.

If you want to export only one layer, select that layer in the Layers palette. Then choose File→Export→Layers as Files. In the box that appears, choose SWF in the Format pop-up menu at the bottom of the box. If you wish to export multiple layers, hold down the Shift key as you select layers in the Layers palette. The export-to-Flash feature does not work in Photoshop; you must use ImageReady.

Extract Background

One compelling effect you can apply to an image, is to erase or extract the background of the image. For example, the picture of a person on the Web page in Figures 6.3 and 6.4 was taken against a normal outdoor background. Scanning the picture and using it as is would produce a regular rectangular image with the background showing. Removing the background gives the picture an irregular and more interesting shape. Removing the background also removes the distracting visual elements, thus placing more importance on the person in the picture.

If you have access to the companion Web site for this book, use those files for the following activity.

There are several methods for removing a background. First, make a duplicate layer so that your original image will be intact if you need it later. If you have a large expanse of a solid color in the background, you might try using the Magic Wand selection tool to select the color and then delete it. Experiment with the

Tolerance settings in the Options bar for the Magic Wand. You might also use the Eraser tool. Magnify your image so that you can see what you are doing up close. Choose a soft-edged brush. Draw with the brush along the edges of the part of the picture you want to keep. If you have well-defined edges, you might try the Background Eraser tool. It automatically finds and deletes any background pixels that do not fit with the edges of the picture you are keeping.

Figure 8.6 shows that the edges of the background around the person were removed first with the Eraser tool. Then the Magic Wand tool was used to select parts of the remaining background. Those parts can then be deleted using the Delete key on the keyboard.

Figure 8.6 Removing the Background of an Image

You could also use a tool called Extract in the Filter menu. When you choose the Extract command, a box appears with several tools that allow you to mark the edges of the area you wish to retain. Use Photoshop's Help menu to learn more about the use of tools for erasing or extracting the background of an image.

☆ SHORTCUT **Magnify or Reduce an Image**

To quickly magnify or reduce your image so that you can see what you are doing up close, use the Control (Command) key while you press the ⊞ or ⊟ keys at the top or right side of your keyboard.

Tools, Tips, and Techniques

☆ **TIP**   **Seeing What You've Missed When Erasing a Background**

Usually when you erase the background, the new background of your image will be transparent. Sometimes it is hard to see if you erased everything. If so, create a new layer and move it underneath your image. Fill it with a bright, contrasting color like pink or yellow. Then, while you are erasing, it will be easier to see areas you missed.

Feathering

Feathering allows you to soften the edges of a selection you've made with the Marquee tools, the Lasso tool, and the Magic Wand. When you choose one of those tools, you can add a value—expressed in number of pixels—to the Feather box on the Options bar. If you've already made a selection, you can choose Feather in the Select menu. When you enter a number, the edges of your selection will be blurred by that many pixels when you move, copy, paste, or fill the selection. This allows you to make soft, natural-looking edges on your images.

File Browser

Once you acquire a large number of images, it becomes difficult to find the one in particular you are looking for. Photoshop's File Browser, available in versions 7 and later, can really help. Open the File Browser by choosing Browse from the File menu. In Photoshop CS, you can toggle the File Browser on and off using the button to the immediate left of the Docking Bar or Palette Well. (The button shows a file folder with a magnifying glass.) In Photoshop 7, the File Browser is a tab on the Docking Bar or Palette Well. Click the tab to toggle it on or off. When the File Browser is open, you will see a Folder list in the top left corner. You can click folders to navigate to one that contains the images you wish to browse through. Once you select a folder, the images will appear as thumbnails on the right side of the File Browser. You can double click a thumbnail to open that image. Hold down the [Shift] key to select and open more than one image.

File Size

A good rule of thumb regarding the file size of the GIFs and JPGs you create for your Web page is that 1 KB of file size equals 1 second of download time. If you add up the file sizes of your Web page images, you will have a good idea of how long it will take to download your page over a slow connection. Keep your file sizes as small as possible by using the Optimize settings in Photoshop's Save for Web box and in the Optimize palette in ImageReady.

File size is directly related to physical size and resolution. Images with a physical size of over 3 inches wide or high will usually have a large file size. Images with a resolution of more than 72 pixels per inch will have a large file size and may also have a large physical size. Pay attention to these factors when producing your images. Use the Image→Image Size box in Photoshop to check on the physical size and resolution of your images.

Tools, Tips, and Techniques

Ideally, your entire Web page should total no more than 50 KB. Most of this total will be taken up by the images on your page. Many designers try to keep their GIFs and JPGs well under 10 KB each, depending on how many images are on the page.

File sizes are measured in bytes, kilobytes, and megabytes. Their relationship to each other, and their abbreviations are as follows:

1024 bytes = 1 kilobyte (1 KB)

1024 kilobytes = 1 megabyte (1 MB)

Full Screen Mode

Sometimes it becomes difficult to get a good idea of how your image looks when you have so many menu bars, palettes, and toolboxes obscuring the view. To see a full-screen view of your image against a black background, click the Full Screen Mode button at the bottom of the Toolbox above the Jump To button. When you do so, your image will appear on a black background. To temporarily remove the toolbox and palettes, press the [Tab] key on your keyboard. If you have rulers showing, you can turn them off by typing [Control]-[R] (Command [⌘]-[R] for Mac) on your keyboard. You can even edit your image in Full Screen Mode. First, select the tool you want to use and the layer you are editing. Then go ahead and edit while you are in the Full Screen Mode.

Gradients

Use the Gradient tool in the Toolbox to create graduated blends of color for a section of an image or for an entire background. First choose two colors for the Foreground and Background Colors at the bottom of the Toolbox. Then choose the Gradient tool. Notice in the Options bar that the dropdown menu at the top left includes several prebuilt gradient styles. Some of the prebuilt gradients use the colors you've chosen. Select a gradient style from the dropdown box. Make duplicate layers or new layers so that you do not ruin your image unintentionally. Then click and drag on a layer. Experiment to produce attractive effects. Notice the graduated background in Figure 8.4.

Grayscale

For the activities in this book, we use the RGB image mode. You can create compelling images using the Grayscale mode as well:

1. Open a color image and use Save As to create a copy of it.

2. With the copy open, choose Image➔Mode➔Grayscale. The color in your image will be removed, and you will see variations of gray instead. (If you have multiple layers, they will be merged when you convert to grayscale. This is why you should make a copy of your image to experiment with.)

3. Choose Image➔Mode➔RGB in the Image menu so that the color palettes will again become available.

4. Make a new layer, and choose a Foreground Color. Decide which portion of the image you want to paint.

5. On the new layer, paint on top of the original image. For example, if you have a picture of a vase of flowers, you might make the entire picture grayscale but then overpaint the individual flowers with the color red.

A similar technique would involve using a color copy of the image along with a grayscale copy. Extract part of the image from the background of the color image, and then copy/paste it into the grayscale image. In the example shown in Figure 8.7, one of the peppers was extracted from a color copy of the image and then pasted into the grayscale image. The final effect of these techniques can be quite compelling.

Figure 8.7 Combination Grayscale and RGB Image

Healing Brush

The Healing Brush tool in Photoshop is similar to the Clone Stamp tool. You can use the Healing Brush to correct or change an area of an image. For example, you might want to touch up a person's face by removing the circles under their eyes. Using the Healing Brush you can draw onto the eye area a sample from some other area of the face. Unlike the Clone Stamp tool, however, the Healing Brush uses the same light, texture, and shading that is present in the portion of the image you are painting onto rather than that of the sampled area. The resulting painted area should blend in seamlessly with the rest of the image.

Inverse–Selecting

Sometimes it is useful to select the **inverse**—or opposite—of an area that you have selected. To do so, make a selection with one of the Selection tools. Then choose Inverse in the Select menu at the top of the screen. The opposite area will become selected. This technique can be useful when you are extracting a part of an image from its background. Use the Eraser tool to erase around the edges of an image you want to keep. Now hold down the Control (Command) key while you click on the layer containing the image you are keeping. You should see that a selection is made around the retained image. In the Select menu at the top of the screen, choose Inverse. The opposite area will be selected. Press the Delete key on your keyboard. All parts of the background around the image will be deleted.

Lasso Tools–Polygon and Magnetic Tools

You learned to use the basic Lasso tool in Chapter Five. If you click and hold the Lasso tool icon in the Toolbox, a fly-out menu appears with additional Lasso tool choices. The Polygon Lasso tool allows you to create a path around the image you are selecting. The Magnetic Lasso tool automatically snaps to the strongest edges of the image you are selecting. Click to set a starting point, release the mouse and move to another area, click again to set a point, and so on. To close your path, click the top of the starting point to release the tool. You may also try drawing with the tools in a freehand motion rather than clicking, stopping, clicking again, and so on. You will need steady mouse skills to make precise selections. In all cases, you can set additional options for the tools in the Options bar.

Layer Comps

Many times, a designer will create multiple versions of a design before deciding on the final one. Photoshop CS contains a new feature called Layer Comps that let you save *snapshots* of particular layer arrangements. Use Layer Comps to view multiple versions of the same Photoshop document. To create a layer comp, choose Window→Layer Comp. The Layer Comp palette will appear. In the triangle menu at the top right of the palette, choose New Layer Comp. In the box that appears, name the layer comp and add comments. (For example, Name: Blue Background; Comments: This version has a blue background instead of a red one.) If you have several layer comps and you wish to view a particular one, select it in the Layer Comp palette and use the triangle menu to Apply Layer Comp. The features of that layer comp will appear in your document window. If you make a change to a layer comp, use the triangle menu to Update Layer Comp.

Liquify

ImageReady contains a Filter tool called Liquify that you can use to create some amazing effects. Create a shape or use an existing image. From the Filter menu, choose Liquify. In the box that appears, use the tools in the upper left corner to drag on your image. It will warp into different shapes, depending on the tools you used. To liquify text, you have to *rasterize* it first. For more information, see "Rasterizing Text Layers" on page 173.

Live Text

As you design a Web page, be sure to include plenty of areas for **live text**. The more live text you have, the faster your page will download and the more searchable and accessible it will be. Save the image elements of your page for the areas where you really want to attract the viewer's attention, such as headlines and subheads. Use images for buttons so that you can create compelling Rollover effects. When you use live text, you can never be quite sure how it will look on any given computer monitor. Test your Web pages on several different monitors and browsers to see if you need to make changes to the font or layout of your page. And remember that live text is about 24% larger on a Windows monitor than on a Mac monitor.

Locking Layers

Once you are finished working on a particular layer and you wish to avoid any accidental changes to it, you can **lock** it. To lock a layer, first select the layer and then click the Lock All icon at the top of the Layers palette—it looks like a padlock. You can also choose to partially lock a layer. Use the icons to the left of the Lock All icon to lock only the Transparency, the Image Pixels, or the Position of the contents.

Master Originals Folder

This concept was mentioned frequently in the first part of this book. But it's worth mentioning again, because so many beginners edit their one-and-only copy of an image. Later, they are often disappointed when they do not have the original, unedited image.

Whenever you acquire an image, put it in a folder called Master Originals. Never edit these images. Always make a copy of an image when you wish to do some editing. Use Photoshop's Save As command to put a copy in a Projects folder for the particular project you are working on.

Merging Layers

Sometimes it is useful to **merge** two or more layers. For example, you may have used a Shape and a Style to create a button layer. The Text layer for the button is separate. Once you are satisfied with all elements you have created, you can choose Merge in the Layer menu at the top of the page to merge the text layer into the shape layer. Once you do so, the text will no longer be editable, so be careful. You may want to use duplicate layers or a copy of the document while you experiment.

If you merge all the layers in an image, your image is considered **flattened**.

Opacity

You can set the **opacity**—or transparency—of any layer. When you choose to lower the opacity of a layer from 100% to a lower number, a portion of the layer below will show through. You can use this technique to create interesting effects, especially when used in conjunction with Blending Modes. In the box next to the word Opacity at the top of the Layers palette, type a number, or use the slider bar to set the opacity of a layer.

Pattern Maker

You can use Photoshop's Pattern Maker to create a tiled background for your Web page. Open an image that includes a section you would like to use as a tiled background. Make a copy of the layer that the section is in. With the copied layer selected, choose Pattern Maker from the Filter menu. A box will appear that includes a selection tool you can use to select part of the image. Once it is selected, click Generate in the top right of the screen. If you are satisfied with the results, click OK. Notice that the tiled background replaces your original layer. This is why you probably want to make a copy of the layer before you begin. You can experiment with the settings in the Pattern Maker box to try different techniques. Image Ready's *Tile Maker* is a similar tool. See "Tile Maker" on page 175.

Quick Mask

Masking part of an image lets you protect it while you apply effects to the image. *Masks* and their related feature, *alpha channels,* can be complex and time-consuming to learn, so you should approach them after you have some experience with Photoshop. However, Photoshop includes a Quick Mask mode that is fairly easy for beginners to learn.

Following are instructions for creating an interesting border around an image, using the Quick Mask mode:

1. Open an image in Photoshop.

2. In the Toolbox, double-click the Edit in Quick Mask Mode button below the Background paint chip. Choose Selected Areas in the box that appears, and click OK.

3. In the Toolbox, choose the Edit in Standard Mode button to the left of the Quick Mask Mode button.

4. Select the layer containing the image.

5. Use one of the Marquee selection tools to select a part of your image.

6. Click the Edit in Quick Mask Mode button. If you have done everything correctly so far, you should see a colored overlay (probably red) on top of the selected part of your image.

7. In the Filter menu, choose Brush Strokes➔Sprayed Strokes. Adjust the settings if you wish (if you make the Stroke Length a large number like 15, it will be easier to see the result) and click OK. You will see that the stroked edges have been applied to the selected area.

8. Click the Edit in Standard Mode button. You will see that the marching ants depict the selected area that includes the brush strokes you applied with the Filter.

9. Choose Inverse from the Select menu. Use the ⌐Delete¬ key on your keyboard to delete the outside border that you no longer want.

10. You will see the stroked edges around the area of the image you selected. Experiment with different filters and different settings.

Rasterizing Text Layers

There are times when you would like to apply paint or a filter to a word or line of text. These tools are not available for normal text layers. In order to use these tools, you must first **rasterize** the text layer. When you rasterize a text layer it is converted to a normal layer, and you can no longer edit the text with the Text tool. When you are ready to rasterize a text layer, select the layer. In the Layer menu at the top of the screen, choose Rasterize➔Type. Now you will be able to use paint, filters, and certain other techniques on the text.

Figure 8.8 shows an image created with several techniques. The text was rasterized and then a color gradient was painted onto the text. The text was then warped with the Liquify filter. The Quick Mask mode and Sprayed Strokes filter were applied to the edges of the photo to create an interesting border.

Figure 8.8 Image with Text That Was Rasterized and Liquified, and a Border That Was Created with the Quick Mask Tool

Red Eye Correction

Use the Color Replacement tool in Photoshop CS and later versions to correct the red eyes that often result from digital cameras. Open the image and use the Zoom tool to magnify the eyes. Select the Color Replacement tool—available from the fly-out menu on the Healing Brush tool, which is the fourth tool down on the left side of the Toolbox. From the Options bar, choose a Brush size that is a bit smaller than the red portion of the eye. Also in the Options bar, make sure the Mode is set to Color. Leave the other options at their default values and experiment with them later. In the Toolbox, choose a Foreground Color. Probably black is best, but you can experiment with other colors. Drag your mouse over the red portion of the eye and it will be replaced with the Foreground Color. For more details on the options available, see "Color Replacement Tool" in this chapter.

Retouching Tools

Photoshop and ImageReady contain six Retouching tools that will help you make corrections and enhancements to your images:

 ☆ *Smudge*: This tool moves pixels of color in the direction in which you drag with your mouse. You might use it to cover up an unwanted spot in the background of an image.

 ☆ *Blur*: A useful application for this tool is to choose a medium to large soft-edged brush and blur the background of an image. This will help make the text or object in the foreground of the image stand out.

 ☆ *Sharpen*: In a small image in which a person appears to blend too much with the background, use this tool to sharpen the face and any other important features. Beware of using too much Sharpen or the image will begin to look unnaturally digital.

 ☆ *Dodge*: Dodging is a photographer's darkroom technique. Use the Dodge tool when you want to lighten part of an image.

 ☆ *Burn*: Burning is also a photographer's darkroom technique. Use the Burn tool when you want to darken part of an image.

 ☆ *Sponge*: Use the Sponge tool to deepen, or saturate, the color in part of an image. You can also use this tool to dilute, or desaturate, the color. Use the Mode pop-up menu in the Options bar to set this tool to Saturate or Desaturate.

Style Guide

When you create a Web design in Photoshop or ImageReady, you should make notes about the elements of your design—a **style guide**. Write down the hexa-decimal and/or RGB codes of the colors you used. Make notes of the various fonts and font sizes you used. Note the sizes of the pictures that appear in the page. If you document as much information as possible, you can work quickly and effi-ciently when you return later to modify a design or create new pages for the site.

Getting into the habit of documentation will eventually lead you to an advanced Web site design technique called CSS, or Cascading Style Sheets. When you use CSS in a Web site, you have to write code only once for things like font sizes, live text link colors, link Rollover colors, and so on. CSS is becoming a preferred technique for Web sites, and you can start to become familiar with this issue by creating your own style guides.

Once you learn more about CSS, you can use the Generate CSS feature in the Slices section of the Output Settings box in ImageReady when you are saving a complete Web page.

Tile Maker

ImageReady's Tile Maker is similar to Photoshop's Pattern Maker. Open an image, and choose Filter→Other→TileMaker. Here is one technique you can use: Click the Kaleidoscope Tile option and click OK. Again choose Filter→Other→ TileMaker. This time, click Blend Edges and set Width at 10%. Also click to Resize Tile to Fill Image. Click OK. From the File menu, choose Output Settings→Background and click to choose View Document as Background. In the File menu, choose Preview In and choose your Web browser to see what the tiled background will look like on a Web page. Experiment with different settings and different images.

Web Photo Gallery

You can use Photoshop to create an instant Web site that features your GIF and JPG images. Use the Web Photo Gallery feature to help you stay organized or to show your images to others. When you create a gallery, Photoshop will make small thumbnail images of each of the images in a particular folder. These thumbnails will appear on the home page of the gallery Web site. When you click one of the thumbnails, you are taken to another page where the full-size version of the image appears. To create a Web photo gallery, choose Automate→Web Photo Gallery from the File menu at the top of the screen. In the box that appears, select the folder that contains the images you want to use. Experiment with the other settings in the box to change the size of the thumbnails and full-size images, and to create custom color combinations for backgrounds and links.

☆ **WARNING**   **Use GIFs and JPGs for the Web Photo Gallery**

Web browsers cannot display Photoshop and ImageReady PSD images. Use the GIFs and JPGs you've created for your Web site. Or use the JPG images that come directly from your digital camera.

WBMP Format for Cell Phones and PDAs

Many cell phones and personal digital assistants (PDAs) are connected wirelessly to the Internet. If you are creating a Web page that requires that the images be optimized in the standard WBMP format, you can use ImageReady to create the images. In the Optimize palette, instead of choosing GIF or JPG, choose WBMP. You can then adjust the Dither and Diffusion options to optimize your image.

◎◎ Web Site Design Do's and Don'ts

Here are two lists of items related to the design of your Web page. You should avoid items on the Don'ts list and do everything you can to employ the ideas and techniques on the *Do's* list:

Design Do's

✔ White space

✔ Readable text

✔ Buttons that are clickable

✔ Things that move—but not too many. Use button Rollovers and animations to spice up your Web site.

✔ Content is king. Sometimes snazzy designs make Web sites unusable.

✔ Styles and themes that are based in symbolism and metaphor from the content

✔ Alt Text. Don't you want everyone to *see* your site?

✔ Inviting home pages that build anticipation. Don't put everything you've got on the home page; make the viewer want to click and go inside.

✔ Simple, tasteful, elegant, *usable* designs

✔ Include a "last modified" date and a contact name and address.

✔ TEST, TEST, TEST!

Design Don'ts

✘ Massive amounts of text

✘ Lots of text in all caps

✘ Text that is unreadable because the background is too busy

✘ Items that look as if they should be clickable but are not. Don't underline words on a Web page—underlining on the Web means clickable.

✘ Impossible navigation. Unless you are creating some kind of a game, make your links and buttons obvious to the viewer.

✘ Graphics that say, "This page is Under Construction." The Web is always under construction. That's why it is so popular and useful.

✘ Ugly color choices

✘ Boring designs that look like everyone else's Web page

✘ Pages that do not appear correctly in different browsers. You forgot to test!

☆ Summary

➤ Remember to use the Photoshop and ImageReady Help menus when you forget something or want to learn something new.

➤ There are many tools, tips, and techniques that will help you create compelling images and Web pages. Some are simple and some are complex. Learn at your own pace, and don't be afraid to experiment.

☆ Online References

Adobe's Advanced Tutorials
`http://www.adobe.com/products/tips/photoshop.html`

The National Association of Photoshop Professionals
`http://www.photoshopuser.com/`

Links to Photoshop Tutorials from About.com
`http://graphicssoft.about.com/cs/photoshop/`

Drop Cap Fonts
`http://fonts.lordkyl.net/fonts.php?category=init`

☆ Review Questions

1. Name two instances where you might use Photoshop or ImageReady actions.
2. Why would you use a contact sheet?
3. What can you do with the Healing Brush?
4. What is the main difference between live text on a Windows computer and a Mac computer?
5. Why would you use a Web Photo Gallery?

☆ Hands-On Exercises

If you have access to the companion Web site for this book, use those files for the exercises.

1. Choose an image that covers the canvas. Add a drop shadow to the image. Notice that the drop shadow exceeds the boundaries of the canvas and thus is not visible. Enlarge the canvas to include the shadow. Crop appropriately and save for the Web.

2. Use ImageReady to create a quick, rough Web site with three or more pages. Organize the pages and images in a folder. Check your directory structure against that shown in Figure 8.3.

3. Choose an image and remove the background using the Eraser, Marquee tools, and Magic Wand. Choose another image and use the Extract Background filter. Compare the techniques and results.

4. Select part of an image and add a feather amount. Copy and Paste into a new document. Repeat this procedure with different feather amounts. Note the differences in the results.

5. Create a background tile using Photoshop's Pattern Maker. Create another background using ImageReady's Tile Maker. Compare the techniques and results.

APPENDIX: ANSWERS TO ODD-NUMBERED REVIEW QUESTIONS

◎ Chapter One

1. Here are six ways to create an image in Photoshop. (1) Start with a blank page and use Photoshop's tools to paint, draw, add text, and apply effects. (2) Open an image from a clip art or photo collection. (3) Open an image saved from the Web. (4) Open a screenshot captured from a computer. (5) Scan a photo, drawing, or object. (6) Download an image from a digital camera.

3. Web designers work with the RGB, Indexed, and Grayscale color modes. "RGB" stands for red, green, and blue, the colors used to make all colors viewed on a television screen or computer monitor. Indexed color is a special palette of a limited set of colors. Grayscale color uses black, white, and shades of gray.

5. Many beginning designers edit their only copy of an image and are disappointed later when they want to use the image without the edits. When you acquire images, put them in a Master Originals folder and do not edit those images. When you have a specific project, make copies of images you wish to use and put them in a Project folder. Your Project images should be saved in the PSD format to take advantage of all of the features of Photoshop. Web pages require JPG and GIF images. Web pages cannot display PSD images.

7. A children's Web site might use bright primary colors. A bank's Web page may require dark or serious colors like blue and gray. A landscaping company's Web site might use "earthy" colors like shades of green, brown, and blue. A race car Web site might use red, black, and yellow—colors commonly used in race car motifs.

◎ Chapter Two

1. It is always best to acquire images at the highest possible quality and save them as Master Originals. You can then make copies of the originals and change the quality settings depending on how you will use the images. For example, you may want to make an image for your Web site. You may also want to use the image for a printed brochure. Make one copy of your original and keep the dpi at 150 for printing. Make another copy of your original and change the dpi to 72 for use on the Web.

3. When you enlarge an image with Photoshop, the quality may be degraded because the same pixels are reproduced to create the enlargement. But if you scan an image at a larger scale setting, you will be acquiring additional pixels, thus creating a higher-quality image.

5. A pixel is the smallest unit of measurement for television screens and computer monitors. There are about 72 pixels in every inch of the screen or monitor. Images for use on the Web should be prepared at 72 pixels per inch; this is referred to as the resolution of the image. If you change the resolution of an image, you will most probably be changing the number of pixels in the image. The term *resolution* is also used in for the screen settings for a computer monitor. Today, most computer monitors use a resolution of at least 800 pixels wide by 600 pixels high.

7. Photographs and other images with subtle shadings or gradations of color should be saved in the JPG format.

◎◎ Chapter Three

1. Raster images (sometimes called bitmap images) are made up of pixels; each pixel has a color and a specific location in the image. Vector images (sometimes called objects) are made up of lines and curves that are based on mathematical formulas.

3. The Shape tools should be used to create vector graphics—sometimes called objects or drawn graphics. A vector graphic contains crisp edges. An area outlined by a vector can be filled with color. A vector graphic can be enlarged to any size without degrading the image. The Painting tools should be used to create raster or bitmap graphics. A raster graphic is a painted image. The edges can become fuzzy when the image is enlarged.

5. A GIF image can contain a maximum of 256 colors.

7. Contrast is one of the most important elements of good design. As you work with color, text, and shapes, use contrasting techniques such as light and dark, big and small, thick and thin, soft and hard, and so on.

◎◎ Chapter Four

1. On a Web page, text that is part of an image file is embedded in the page. The image, including the text, will appear exactly as it was created. We call this *image text. Live text* is typed into Web page editing software or typed directly within the code of an HTML document. Live text uses the fonts from the user's computer. Live text may appear differently on different computers.

3. To increase readability, use a sans serif font for large bodies of dense text on the Web.

5. Whenever you create a new image with a white or colored background, the bottommost layer is automatically named Background. This layer has some special properties that are useful for advanced techniques. The Background layer cannot be moved. You can rename the Background layer by double-clicking on it and entering a new name. When you do this, you will make it a Normal layer, and it can be moved.

7. Once you decide on a particular look—or style—for your Web buttons, you can save the settings as a custom style. You will then have the custom style available as you continue to work on additional pages and images. If a long time elapses between design sessions, and you forget which settings you originally used, having saved a custom style will assure uniformity in your design. It is important that you do not change the style of your navigation buttons on different pages of your Web site lest you confuse the viewers.

9. You can use the Show/Hide Layers feature to create a set of multiple buttons within one Photoshop document. For example, when you are saving a series of Web page buttons with different sets of text, you might create a Shape layer for the button and three additional layers, each with different text. Turn off two of the Text layers and save a GIF file. Then turn on a different Text layer and save another GIF. Repeat. You will now have three GIF files for your Web page, each with the same button shape but with different text on top. This helps to assure uniformity in the look of all of your buttons. It is also an efficient way to work, because all of the necessary files are contained in one document.

◎◎ Chapter Five

1. When you are creating an animation in ImageReady, first use the Layers palette to create the layers that contain the images that will be used in the animation. Then use the Animation palette to create frames to animate the series of images over a period of time. In each frame you will show or hide particular layers to achieve the animation effect.

3. Tweened frames are steps in the progress of an animation. You can create your own tweened frames or you can use the Tween menu in the Animation palette. Tweened frames change the image in gradual steps between the first frame and the last. Using tweened frames with interim edits creates a fluid motion and makes an animation appear more realistic.

5. In an animation along a path, an image moves across, around, up, or down. For example, a bird flies across the screen.

◎◎ Chapter Six

1. The basic components of a Web page are text, links, and images.

3. Designers use the visual notion of a table with rows and columns in the design process. Tables help you decide where to put the elements of a design. Tables are also a fundamental part of Web design. Not only are tables helpful for the general design concept, but Web editing programs use actual tables to control the layout of a Web page design.

5. Most navigation bars appear at the top or the left side of a Web page.

◎◎ Chapter Seven

1. Slicing a large Web page image into smaller pieces makes the image download faster in the Web browser. You can also use the slicing technique to separate the Web page buttons in a design. When you separate the buttons, you can apply effects such as Rollover behaviors to each separate button.

3. Once your design is complete, drag your mouse out from the vertical and horizontal rulers to create guides—thin, blue lines that denote the areas to be sliced. For example, put guides at the top, bottom, and sides of a rectangular button. Then press the Create Slices from Guides command in the Slices menu at the top of the screen. The slices will then be automatically created.

5. Image maps allow you to make any portion of an image a link to a URL. Unlike rectangular images or slices, an image map can be almost any shape. Thus, you can designate an irregularly shaped image or portion of an image to be a clickable link.

◎◎ Chapter Eight

1. There are many prebuilt actions you can experiment with. Some create interesting text effects, such as Flaming Text or Wood Frame. In addition, you might use an action to change the resolution of a series of images from 150 dpi to 72 dpi for the Web. Whenever you have to perform the same technique or set of techniques on a batch of images, you should record an action to use on each image to save time and effort.

3. The Healing Brush allows you to sample one part of an image and paint with it on another part of the image. The Healing Brush uses the same light, texture, and shading that is present in the portion of the image you are painting onto, rather than that of the sampled area. The resulting painted area should blend in seamlessly with the rest of the image.

5. Making a Web Photo Gallery is an easy way to create an instant Web site that displays your GIF and JPG images. For example, you might want to create a Web Photo Gallery to display pictures from your vacation and share them with your family and friends. The first page of a Web Photo Gallery includes small thumbnail images. Because the images are small they will download quickly. A viewer who wishes to see a larger version of the image can click on the thumbnail to enlarge it. The large images will take longer to download. A Web Photo Gallery is a complete Web site; you can customize various aspects of the elements of the site.

INDEX

A

Actions, 158–159
Adjustments, 32
   Auto Contrast, 33
   Auto Levels, 32
   and Sketch/Chrome
     Filter, 41
   Hue/Saturation, 34
   Levels, 33
Adobe Go Live, 118, 135,
   141
Adobe Illustrator, 50
Airbrush tool, 63
Alt text, 143
Animation, 93–113
   animated advertising
     banner, 96–97
   animated GIF image, 94
   basic principles, 94
   creating a basic
     animation, 96–104
   creating a complex
     animation, 104–108
   creating frames, 99
   deleting frames, 102
   duplicate current frame,
     100
   timing, 103
   tween, 101–102
Animation along a path,
   106
Animation in place, 105
Animation palette, 99–100
   Select Looping Options,
     103
Automate
   Contact Sheet, 160
   Crop and Straighten, 32
   Web Photo Gallery, 175

B

Background
   in creating new images,
     14, 56
   transparent image
     backgrounds, 64
   graphics and tiles,
     126–127
   full-screen backgrounds,
     127
   tiled, 128–129
   saving background colors
     or images, 151–152
Background Layer, 78
Bitmap images (*See* Raster
   images)
Blending Modes, 159
Blur tool (*See* Retouching
   tools)
Border, 41–42
Browsers
   and common monitor
     sizes, 47, 120
Brush tool
   and color, 12
   painting on a new
     image, 15
   changing the size, 15
Burn tool (*See* Retouching
   tools)

C

CSS (*See* Cascading Style
   Sheets)
Canvas, 2, 62, 160
Cascading Style Sheets,
   174–175
Cells, 120
Character palette, 76
Clip Art, 29
Clone Stamp Tool, 43–44

Color
   harmony, 13
   modes, 7
   palette, 10
   picker, 8, 9, 16
   saving in Swatches
     palette, 17
   schemes, 15–16
   selection tools, 8
   values, 13
Color Guide
   creating a guide, 13
   choosing harmonious
     colors, 16
   saving the colors in, 17
   and Web design, 117
Color Replacement tool, 160
Color Table
   and GIF images, 52
CMYK color mode, 7
Commit button
   to finalize a
     transformation, 63
   to finalize text, 74
Composite image, 87
Compression, 45
Constrain proportions
   in Image Size box, 37–38
   during selection, 42
   and shape tools, 57
Contact Sheet, 160–161
Contrast, 13
Copy merged, 127
Copyright, 44, 47
Crop Tool, 31–32

D

Descreen, 28
Design
   Above the Fold, 124
   and graphic images, 50

general information, 162
planning a Web page, 117
Power of Three, 99
symbols and metaphors
    in, 121
visually dividing the
    design area, 120
Web design basics, 116
Web design do's and
    don'ts, 176
Web page layouts,
    125–126
Directory Structure, 162
Direct Selection Tool, 60
Disjointed Rollovers, 162
Docking Bar, 163
Dodge tool (*See* Retouching
    tools)
Dots per inch, 28
Drawn,drawing (*See also,*
    Vector), 3
Driver for scanner, 28
Drop Caps, 164
Drop Shadow (*See* Effects)
Duplicate layer (*See also,*
    Layers), 165

E
Effects, 82–86
    Bevel and Emboss, 84–85
    Drop shadow, 82–83
    editing, 86
    previewing, 83–84
Enlarge image
    during scanning, 28–29
Eraser tool, 64, 166
Ethics
    using Photoshop
        appropriately, 44
Eyedropper tool, 16
Extension, 20–21
Export to Macromedia Flash
    (SWF), 165
Extract background, 165

F
Feathering, 167

File Browser, 167
File Size, 23, 167
Fill technique, 14–15
Filters
    Artistic/Colored Pencil,
        40
    Artistic/Film Grain, 40
    Blur, 40
    Distort, 40
    Extract, 166
    Glass, 40
    Noise/Add Noise, 40, 89
    Sketch/Chrome, 41
    Stylize/Wind, 41
    Unsharp Mask, 35
Flattened images, 78
Flowchart, 117
Fonts, and Web design, 118
Format
    of saved images, 17–18
    Photoshop or PSD, 18,
        30
Frames (*See* Animation)
Full Screen Mode, 168

G
GIF (*See also,* Format)
    and indexed color, 51
    and Color Table, 52
    animated, 94
    purpose of, 18
    saving for the Web, 23
    transparency, 54
Gradient tool, 88–89
Gradients, 168
Grayscale
    color mode, 7
    painting with color,
        168–169
Guide tool, 121
    creating guides, 121
    to denote the fold, 124
Guides
    creating guides, 137
    viewing/showing guides,
        136

H
Halo
    and transparent images,
        65
Healing Brush, 169
Help menu, 158
Hexadecimal, 12
Hide, 6
Histogram and Levels
    adjustments, 33
How To Tips, 158
Hypertext Markup
    Language (*See* HTML)
HTML
    and Web–Safe Color, 11
    and live text, 70
    and Web page design,
        118
    writing basic code,
        145–146

I
Image, 2
    creating a new image, 14
    size and resolution, 35
    composite, 87
Image Maps, 149–150
ImageReady, 2–3
    Previewing a background
        tile, 128
    Tabs at top of document
        window, 110
    Toolbox, 137
    using ImageReady, 95
    Work Area, 96
ImageReady Output settings
    for backgrounds, 128
    setting the options, 151
    and TileMaker, 175
Image Size box, 36–37
    Pixel dimensions, 38
    Document Size, 38
Image sizes
    common for the Web, 39
    and digital photographs,
        39
Import, 28

Indexed color, 7
    and GIF files, 51
Info palette, 56
Inverse, selecting, 170

J

JPG (*See also*, Format)
    purpose of, 18
    saving for the Web,
        44–46
    and JPEG, 45
Jump To button, 95–96

K

Kerning, 76

L

Layers, 3, 77–81
    adding,78
    deleting, 79
    duplicating, 81, 108
    effects, 82
    locking, 171
    merging, 171
    moving, 81
    naming, 80
    selecting, 80
    showing and hiding, 80
    style, 82
Layer Comps, 170
Layer Sets, 106–107
Linked Layers, 106–107
Layout
    newspaper, magazine,
        book, 122
    sketching designs,
        125–126
Leading, 76
Liquify, 170
Live Text (*See also*, Text),
    171
Locking Layers, 171

M

Macromedia Dreamweaver,
    118, 135, 141
Macromedia Flash, 50

Macromedia Freehand, 50
Marching ants
    and Crop tool, 32
Master Originals Folder
    and saving strategy, 19
    and saving a copy of an
        image, 30–31
    rationale for, 36
    general information, 171
Matte, 65
Menu bar, 4
Merging layers, 171
Metaphors, 116, 121
Mickey Mouse, 94
Microsoft Front Page, 118,
    135, 141
Millions of Colors, 28
Moiré pattern when
    scanning, 29
Monitors, computer
    resolution and the Web,
        39
    determining Web page
        size, 118
Move tool
    moving image to
        another document, 98

N

Naming guidelines for
    images and folders, 19
Navigation, 123

O

Objects (*See* Vector images)
Opacity
    and layers, 90
    general information, 171
Optimize
    and the Save for Web
        box, 21
    and ImageReady palette,
        95, 109
    and Animation Palette,
        109
    slices, 146–147
Options bar, 4–5

and Magic Wand tool, 42
    and Text tool, 73
Output images, 20

P

Painted, painting (*See also*,
    Raster), 3
Palettes, 6
Palette Well (*See* Docking
    Bar)
Paragraph palette, 76
Pattern Maker, 172
Pencil tool, 63
Pen tool, 56
    drawing linear shapes,
        58
    drawing curves, 58–59
    freeform pen tool, 59
    refining paths, 59–60
Photoshop Work Area, 4
Pixar Studios, 94, 112
Pixel, 6, 35
Pixels per inch, 36
Preferences
    Transparency and
        Gamut, 54
    Units and Rulers, 6–7
Project folder, 19, 30–31
PSD (*See* Format)

Q

Quality
    and Save for Web/JPG,
        45
Quick Mask, 172

R

RGB
    color mode, 7
    sliders in Color palette,
        10, 12
Raster images, 50
Rasterize
    and saving a GIF file, 65
    text layers, 173
Red Eye correction, 173
Remote Rollovers, 162

Resample Image
in Image Size box, 37
Resolution
when scanning, 28
and image size, 35–36
and computer monitors,
39
Retouching tools, 174
Rollovers
behavior, 129
disjointed, 162
programming the
behavior, 147–148
Remote, 162
Rollover State, 129–130,
147–148
Prebuilt rollover styles,
148
Rotate Canvas, 31
Rulers
Units and Rulers
Preference setting, 6
toggle on and off, 35
Running Horse, Eadweard
Muybridge, 112

S

Save for Web
settings in Save for Web
box, 21–22
and JPG images, 45
and transparent GIF, 65
and layered image, 90
and animation, 109
Save Menu Commands, 18
Save command, 20
Save As command, 21
Save As a Copy, 30
Save Optimized in
ImageReady, 111
Saving a Web page, 152–153
Saving Slices, 153
Saving strategy, 19
rationale for, 36
Scale Styles in Image Size
box, 37
Scanner and scanning, 28

Selection box and Crop tool,
32
Select Menu, 41
and box of marching
ants, 42
select inverse, 170
Selection tools
Rectangular marquee, 42
Elliptical marquee, 42
Lasso tool, 42
Magic Wand, 42, 166
Single Column, 127
Single Row, 127
Shape Tools, 55–56
Ellipse tool, 56
Custom shape tool, 56, 89
Sharpen tool (*See* Retouching
tools)
Show, 6
Showing layers, 80
Showing and hiding layers
for Rollovers, 130
Showpeg, 131
Size (*See* File Size)
Sketchbook
learning to create images,
50
planning animation, 96
thumbnail sketches, 118
Web design, 116, 120
Slicing a Web page, 136–140
Slices
auto slices, 139
creating, 138
deleting, 139–140
editing, 140
from guides, 139
selecting, 139
user slices, 138–139
viewing, 137
Slice Options, 141–144
Slice tool, 138
Slice select tool, 138, 140
Smudge tool (*See* Retouching
tools)
Spectrum
color palette spectrum, 10

color picker spectrum,
16–17
Splash Screen, 120
Sponge tool (*See* Retouching
tools)
Stock Photography, 29, 47
Style Guide, 174
Styles palette, 56
applying a prebuilt style
to a shape, 61
Styles
and layer effects, 82
custom, 86
Swatches palette, 11
Symbols, 116, 121

T

Table, 120–121
Text
live text on a Web page,
70, 144
image text on a Web
page, 70
on a screen vs. on a
printed page, 71–72
creating, 74
changing properties, 74
orienting, 75
warping, 75
along a path, 75
single line, 76
paragraph, 76
Text tool
and color, 12
using, 72
keyboard shortcut for
selecting, 73
and layers, 73
Tiling, 127
Tile Maker, 175
Toolbox, ImageReady, 137,
198
Toolbox, Photoshop, 4–5,
and inside back cover
Tool Tips, 6
Tracking, 76

Transform tools, 56, 89, 109
  Distort tool, 62
Transparency, 54
  options for GIF files,
    65–66
True Color, 28
Tweening (*See also*,
    Animation), 94
Type (*See* Text)

U
Unsharp Mask (*See* Filters)

V
Vector graphics
  general information, 50

drawing a vector image,
    54–55
View Menu
  show guides and slices,
    136

W
WBMP format, 175
Walt Disney, 94
Web 216 colors, 8, 11, 12
Web page, basic
  components, 116
Web Photo Gallery, 175
Web–Safe color, 11
Web Site Design Do's and
  Don'ts, 176

White space, 116
Window menu, 10
Work Area (*See* Photoshop
  Work Area and/or
  ImageReady Work Area)

Z
Zoom tool
  and Save for Web box, 46
  and magnifying a portion
    of an image, 53, 63

CREDITS

Figure 2.7   photograph courtesy of Terry Farmer Photography

Figures 5.2, 5.3,   Eagle image courtesy Hemera Photo Objects
5.4, 5.5, 5.6, 5.7

Figure 8.4   section of Web page courtesy of the University of Illinois, Chicago

Figure 8.5   © 2003 by the New York Times Co. Reprinted with permission.

Figure 8.8   photograph courtesy of the University of Illinois, Springfield

Web-Safe Colors

Most computers can display millions of colors, but they do not display all colors consistently. For example, one computer may display a Web page with a dark red background, whereas another displays the same Web page with a brown background. To ensure that your Web pages look the same to everyone, select your colors from the following palette of 216 Web-safe colors. These colors will always look the same (or at least very close to the same) on all computer platforms and computer monitors. Chapter One provides an explanation of the RGB and hexadecimal color codes.

THE IMAGEREADY CS® TOOLBOX

Commonly used fly-out menus are shown at the bottom
of this page and are noted in **bold** in the Toolbox.

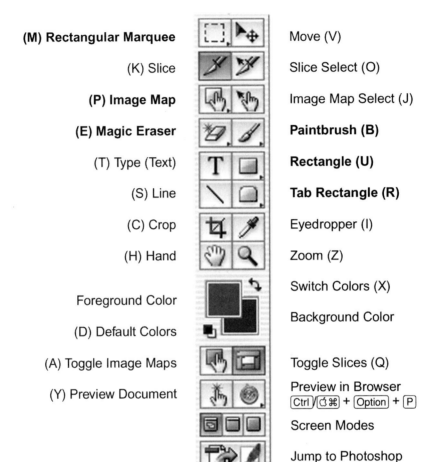

(M) Rectangular Marquee	Move (V)
(K) Slice	Slice Select (O)
(P) Image Map	Image Map Select (J)
(E) Magic Eraser	**Paintbrush (B)**
(T) Type (Text)	**Rectangle (U)**
(S) Line	**Tab Rectangle (R)**
(C) Crop	Eyedropper (I)
(H) Hand	Zoom (Z)
	Switch Colors (X)
Foreground Color	Background Color
(D) Default Colors	
(A) Toggle Image Maps	Toggle Slices (Q)
(Y) Preview Document	Preview in Browser Ctrl /⌘ + Option + P
	Screen Modes
	Jump to Photoshop

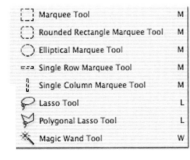

Marquee Tool	M
Rounded Rectangle Marquee Tool	M
Elliptical Marquee Tool	M
Single Row Marquee Tool	M
Single Column Marquee Tool	M
Lasso Tool	L
Polygonal Lasso Tool	L
Magic Wand Tool	W

Rectangle Image Map Tool	P
Circle Image Map Tool	P
Polygon Image Map Tool	P

Magic Eraser Tool	E
Eraser Tool	E

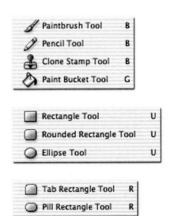

Paintbrush Tool	B
Pencil Tool	B
Clone Stamp Tool	B
Paint Bucket Tool	G

Rectangle Tool	U
Rounded Rectangle Tool	U
Ellipse Tool	U

Tab Rectangle Tool	R
Pill Rectangle Tool	R